# EAT
# YOURSELF
# THIN

# EAT YOURSELF THIN

## SUPERFOODS & RECIPES
## TO BOOST METABOLISM & BURN FAT

GILL PAUL

NUTRITIONIST: KAREN SULLIVAN, ASET, VTCT, BSC

hamlyn

An Hachette UK Company
www.hachette.co.uk

First published in Great Britain in 2014 by Hamlyn,
a division of Octopus Publishing Group Ltd
Endeavour House
189 Shaftesbury Avenue
London WC2H 8JY
www.octopusbooks.co.uk

Distributed in U.S. by Hachette Book Group USA,
237 Park Avenue, New York NY 10017 USA
www.octopusbooksusa.com

Distributed in Canada by Canadian Manda Group,
165 Dufferin Street, Toronto, Ontario,
Canada M6K 3HG

Copyright © Octopus Publishing Group Ltd 2014

ISBN 978-0-60062-702-9

A CIP catalog record for this book is available from
the Library of Congress

Printed and bound in China

10 9 8 7 6 5 4 3 2 1

All reasonable care has been taken in the
preparation of this book but the information
it contains is not intended to take the place of
treatment by a qualified medical practitioner.

People with known nut allergies should avoid
recipes containing nuts or nut derivatives,
and vulnerable people should avoid dishes
containing raw or lightly cooked eggs.

Standard kitchen level spoon and cup
measurements are used in all recipes.
Ovens should be preheated to the specified
temperature—if using a convection oven,
follow the manufacturer's instructions for
adjusting the time and temperature. Medium eggs
should be used unless otherwise stated.

Some of the recipes in this book have previously
appeared in other titles published by Hamlyn.

**Art Director:** Jonathan Christie
**Photographic Art Direction and Prop Styling:**
Isabel de Cordova
**Photography:** Will Heap
**Food Styling:** Gee Charman
**Editors:** Katy Denny & Alex Stetter
**Copy Editor:** Jo Smith
**Assistant Production Manager:** Caroline Alberti

# CONTENTS

# INTRODUCTION

It may seem a strange idea that you can eat yourself thin, when eating made you overweight in the first place. However, it's not the process of eating that causes weight gain, but eating too much of the wrong kinds of foods and drinking the wrong kinds of drinks. This book shows you how to lose weight—and keep it off—by focusing on foods that make your digestive, hormonal, and cardiovascular systems work at optimum level, and on fluids that fully hydrate and replenish you.

Most weight-loss diets starve you. They tell you to cut right back on calories, eliminate carbs, or skip meals—but all of these approaches are almost certain to make you regain the weight you've lost as soon as you stop dieting. The body is designed to maintain itself just the way it is—even if it's overweight. If you cut back drastically on your food intake, your body will compensate by storing more of the calories you do eat as fat. It's a mechanism designed to save your life in times of famine, but it's not so desirable when you've got three months to shape up for a beach vacation.

## How hormones affect weight

Hormones are the key to successful long-term weight loss. Several different hormones govern your appetite and the way your body processes food.

●  **Ghrelin and leptin** A hormone called ghrelin tells the brain when you are hungry and should eat more, while another hormone called leptin tells the brain when you are full. However, these hormones can stop functioning properly in overweight people, making them feel hungry even after eating. To lose weight painlessly, it's essential to get these hunger hormones working effectively.

●  **Insulin** Some foods are more likely to be converted into fat in the body than others because they cause blood sugar levels to rise rapidly, making the body produce insulin (see box, The glycemic index). Insulin is the hormone that converts food into fuel for our muscles, and turns any we don't need into fat to be stored for use another day. High insulin levels make us store more fuel as fat and make us continue to feel hungry even when we've just eaten.

●  **Cortisol** Another hormone that can interfere with weight-loss efforts is cortisol. High levels of cortisol, which is released when we are stressed, cause increased appetite and lead to more fat padding the waistline, as well as making us crave sugary, fatty foods for a quick energy burst. However, these sugary fatty foods will only exacerbate the existing hormonal imbalances.

The way to break the pattern of cravings for unhealthy foods, or weight that piles back on again as soon as you stop dieting, is to get all your hormone levels back into balance. And to achieve that, the last thing you should do is "shock" your body by starving it for a few weeks on a conventional diet. If you want to lose weight, and stay that way, you have to change the types of food you eat, and change them for good.

### The glycemic index and how to control cravings

The glycemic index (GI) rates foods according to their effect on blood sugar. High-GI foods, such as sugar, alcohol, and refined (white) flour products, are broken down quickly by the digestive system and cause blood sugar levels and insulin levels to soar, then plummet. Some people feel jittery and faint when levels drop, and get cravings to eat sugary, refined foods as soon as possible. The way to beat the cravings is to eat low-GI foods, such as whole grains, beans, fruits, and vegetables, all of which will make you feel fuller for longer.

However, if you are a junk food or sugar addict, there is another reason to kick your habit, not just to lose weight. If you eat a lot of high-GI foods, the blood sugar/insulin mechanism can break down and cause insulin resistance, and eventually type-2 diabetes.

## How to eat yourself thin

### 1. Eat regularly

Eat small, regular meals and snacks composed of low-GI foods (whole grains, beans and lentils, vegetables) and high-quality protein (fish, eggs, poultry, lean meat, soy products). These are digested slowly, meaning there is no spike in blood sugar levels and no excess insulin. This will also keep the leptin and ghrelin levels steady so you don't feel hungry. Try to eat something every three hours that you are awake. You'll have good energy levels, and the fiber in the low-GI foods will help to keep your digestive system working efficiently. Optimum digestion is one of the keys to sustained weight loss and overall health.

### 2. Avoid bad fats

Avoid unhealthy saturated fats (found in fatty and processed meats and bakery products containing palm oil) and trans fat (found in spreads and many packaged cookies, cakes, and pastries), but do eat foods containing healthy fats, such as olives, avocado, nuts, seeds, and oily fish. Omega-3 fats found in fish, such as salmon, herring, mackerel, and sardines, can help reduce hunger, as well as be good for your heart and circulatory system.

### 3. Choose soup for lunch

Soup is a nutritious appetite suppressant and an ideal lunch for those who are watching their weight. In studies at Penn State University in Pennsylvania, it was found that ghrelin production was suppressed for at least twice as long in women who had a bowl of chicken and rice soup than in those who ate a chicken and rice casserole.

## 4. Get some sleep

Good-quality sleep is important for those who want to lose weight, because lack of sleep leads to the production of more ghrelin and less leptin, and also disrupts the glucose/insulin metabolism. Try to eat foods containing the amino acid tryptophan, such as chicken, cheese, eggs, oats, and brown rice, to reduce stress and promote restful sleep.

## 5. Avoid processed foods

Cook from scratch as much as possible. Key nutrients are often removed from food when it is processed. Chromium, for example, is an important mineral for maintaining blood sugar and insulin levels, as well as keeping cholesterol at normal levels, but is often removed from foods in processing. Make sure you get enough from your diet by including onions, tomatoes, mushrooms, and whole-grain cereals.

## 6. Look after your organs

The liver filters old hormones from the blood, but it's unable to do this efficiently if it is clogged up and overworked. That's just one of the reasons why drinking a lot of alcohol is not a good idea, whether trying to lose weight or not. Eat foods that support the liver (such as coconut, brown rice, whole grains, root vegetables, and apples) to support your weight-loss efforts, especially if your weight gain is due to menopause or premenstrual syndrome (PMS).

Iodine is crucial for the functioning of the thyroid gland, which determines the metabolic rate. If your thyroid is even slightly underactive, you will gain weight easily and find it difficult to lose again. Good sources of iodine include seaweed, fish, eggs, onions, and artichokes.

## 7. Stay hydrated

Drink plenty of plain water during the day in order to stay hydrated. Herb teas are also good, and green tea can positively help weight loss. Cut right back on caffeine-containing drinks (such as coffee, black tea, and colas) which stimulate the release of insulin.

Pure fruit juices can cause a blood sugar spike because of the fructose they contain, but adding some low-fat yogurt to make a smoothie brings down their GI rating. Avoid all sweetened and sports drinks—even water "with a hint of fruit," which often has a lot of artificial sweetener in it. Be aware that diet foods and drinks often contain high levels of sweeteners. Although they are low in calories, the sweet taste seems to trick your brain into expecting sugar and cause it to release hormones accordingly.

## 8. Treat yourself

Include some treats in your diet. You don't want to feel as though you are living a life of denial. It helps if you choose treats that have some nutritional benefits, such as a couple of squares of semisweet dark chocolate, a fruity dessert, or a small glass of red wine. Avoid junk foods, which are high in saturated fats, trans fats, and sugars without supplying any nutrition at all, and which also place a heavy load on the digestive system.

## Getting started

You'll notice that there's no mention of calories, points, or portion sizes in this book. You won't have to measure precise quantities or sit poring over a calculator to work out whether you are allowed dessert. It's about developing a new relationship with food in which you avoid "empty" calories and become aware of the effects on your body of each food or drink that passes your lips. You may even eat more than you have been doing in the past, because when you consume healthy foods, the body uses them up instead of turning them into fat.

To start losing weight, follow the two-week program on pages 30–33. This will teach you the basics and help you realize that it's not going to be so hard this time. If you have encountered specific problems when trying to lose weight in the past, check the problem solver on pages 26–29. It will tell you which foods to focus on, then you can read pages 12–25 for suggestions about ways you can include them in your diet. All of the foods listed in this book, and used in

the recipes, are designed to promote weight loss in some way, and incorporating them into your diet may be just what you need to jump-start the process.

To give yourself an even better chance of success, start following a regular exercise program, too. Choose something you enjoy. Study after study has shown that dieters who exercise are much more likely to keep the weight off long term. You'll feel better as soon as you start following this healthy eating program, combined with exercising most days. Looking after yourself also boosts self-esteem, so you'll both look and feel great.

## Keeping up the good work

At the end of the two-week program, carry on eating in the same way: have three small meals and three small snacks a day, never letting more than three hours go by without having some nutritious low-GI food.

Don't keep hopping on the bathroom scale, because weight can fluctuate from day to day, but aim for a steady loss of not more than 1–2 lb per week. If you aren't beginning to lose weight after a month of eating healthily, you may need to reduce your portion sizes slightly, but don't make any sudden or drastic changes. Once you reach your target weight, carry on eating exactly as you have been, perhaps slightly increasing your portion sizes. And don't forget to have those treats. You'll find that your tastes will change once you get used to eating healthily and you won't crave heavy, fatty, sugary foods anymore. When your body is working efficiently, maintaining a healthy weight comes naturally.

# THIN
# SUPERFOODS

# SUPERFOODS

These are the key foods to focus on when you want to lose weight. Each one encourages the burning of fat cells and boosts the performance of every system in your body.

## Blueberries

✔ Boost metabolism
✔ Reduce inflammation
✔ Lower cholesterol
✔ Balance blood sugar
✔ Prevent formation of new fat cells

Exciting research suggests that blueberries play a key role in preventing insulin resistance, which is implicated in diabetes and, in particular, belly fat formation. They also help to lower blood pressure and cholesterol.

**They are rich in ...**
→ Fiber, preventing constipation and improving nutrient uptake
→ Polyphenols, which prevent the development of fat cells
→ Anthocyanins, which reduce inflammation and improve health
→ Flavonoids, which boost the metabolism

**Use in ...** breakfast juices and smoothies; bake into crisps, and stir into oatmeal; puree and serve with yogurt; add to whole-grain pancakes; toss into leafy green salads with a handful of toasted hazelnuts and some feta; use dried blueberries in place of raisins in salads, stews, and baked goods.

SEE: GREEN TEA OATMEAL WITH BLUEBERRIES, P. 36; SUMMER BERRY GRANOLA, P. 38; CHICKEN & BLUEBERRY PASTA SALAD, P. 96; BLUEBERRY CHEESECAKE DESSERTS, P. 114; CINNAMON BRIOCHE WITH MIXED BERRIES, P. 124.

# Green tea

✔ Promotes the loss of body fat
✔ Improves metabolism
✔ Encourages a sense of calm
✔ Reduces sugar cravings
✔ Supports liver function
✔ Lowers blood pressure

Green tea is rich in antioxidants that are known to help prevent several types of cancer and enhance metabolism. One study found that men who drank green tea daily had significantly smaller waist measurements, while another found that regular drinkers burn more than 200 extra calories per day than nondrinkers. It supports liver function, improving hormone balance, making it an excellent choice for anyone with hormone-related weight gain.

### It's rich in …

→ Catechins, which encourage the loss of body fat and promote metabolism
→ Theanine, an amino acid that eases feelings of depression and lifts mood
→ Natural ACE inhibitors, which lower blood pressure
→ Antioxidants, supporting an increase good cholesterol and lowering high blood pressure

**Use in …** hot or cold drinks, with lemon, honey, and/or mint; soak rolled oats or muesli in green tea instead of water or milk; blend with berries, honey, and yogurt for a healthy smoothie; soak dried fruit in green tea and serve as a warm compote.

SEE: GREEN TEA OATMEAL WITH BLUEBERRIES, P. 36; GREEN TEA & GINGER GRANITA, P. 120.

# Cider vinegar

✔ Reduces appetite
✔ Encourages healthy digestion
✔ Stimulates metabolism
✔ Stabilizes blood sugar
✔ Prevents abdominal fat forming
✔ Reduces blood pressure

Apple cider vinegar is a natural digestive that can encourage healthy assimilation of food and also stimulate the metabolism. Several studies have found that it helps to lower blood sugar levels and blood pressure, and it leaves you feeling more satisfied and fuller after a meal.

### It's rich in …

→ Acetic acid, which suppresses appetite, prevents fat accumulation (particularly around the belly), and reduces blood pressure
→ Potassium, helping to improve brain and nervous system health, increase alertness, and balance blood sugar levels
→ Pectin, which helps to regulate blood pressure and reduce bad cholesterol
→ Malic acid, which boosts energy levels and promotes liver function, thus balancing hormones

**Use in …** vinaigrettes with honey and olive oil; stir into a glass of hot water with honey; add to tomato sauces, soups, and casseroles to lift flavor; use as a marinade for meat, fish, and poultry; use to pickle beets for a nutrient-rich feast!

SEE: HUEVOS RANCHEROS, P. 50; CRANBERRY & APPLE SMOOTHIE, P. 64; CHILLED GAZPACHO, P. 74; LETTUCE WRAPPERS WITH CRAB, P. 82; CHICKEN BROCHETTES WITH CUCUMBER & KELP SALAD, P. 94; CHICKEN & APPLE STEW, P. 97.

## Soy products

✔ Promotes digestion
✔ Prevents constipation
✔ Balances hormones
✔ Reduces cholesterol
✔ Controls blood sugar levels
✔ Supports heart health

Soy products (in the form of edamame/soybeans, tofu, soy milk, and soy yogurt) are an excellent source of protein, which will help you feel fuller for longer and provide a sustained source of energy. It also contains chemicals that have been shown to reduce the production of fat cells. It is one of only a few plant sources of omega-3 oils, which encourage overall health, and help to balance weight and mood.

**They are rich in ...**

➔ Phytoestrogens, which can balance hormones, thus reducing hormonal bloating and weight gain
➔ Isoflavones, which reduce cholesterol levels and protect your heart
➔ Genistein, which reduces the size and production of fat cells
➔ Peptides, which improve blood pressure, control blood sugar levels, and boost immune function

**Use in ...** salads as steamed edamane (soybeans) with a zesty lime dressing; steam and toss edamame with olive oil, lemon, and black pepper; puree the beans as an alternative to hummus; stir-fry tofu with brightly colored vegetables; serve soy milk or yogurt with oatmeal and fruit.

SEE: ROASTED EDAMAME, P. 56; BAKED TOFU STICKS, P. 58; VEGETABLE & TOFU STIR-FRY, P. 106.

## Parsnips

✔ Balance blood sugar
✔ Encourage healthy digestion
✔ Lower cholesterol
✔ Ease constipation
✔ Reduce high blood pressure
✔ Support thyroid function

The high fiber content of parsnips, along with their sweet taste, helps to reduce hunger and keep you feeling fuller for longer. They are rich in the B vitamins to support balanced moods and aid restful sleep and even ease the impact of stress.

**They are rich in ...**

➔ Folic acid, for a healthy heart and nervous system and balanced moods
➔ Soluble fiber, which lowers cholesterol and helps to balance blood sugar levels
➔ Potassium, helping to regulate blood sugar and boost immunity
➔ Manganese, which is required for healthy thyroid function

**Use in ...** stews, casseroles, and soups with other root vegetables; puree as an accompaniment to fish, poultry, and meat; roast with thyme and a drizzle of olive oil; mash as a topping for fish, chicken, or vegetable casseroles.

SEE: SPLIT PEA & PARSNIP SOUP, P. 72; SPICY CARROT & LEMON SOUP, P. 76; SCALLOP, PARSNIP & CARROT SALAD, P. 84; CHEESY PORK WITH PARSNIP PUREE, P. 102; MOROCCAN CHICKPEAS WITH CARROTS & DATES, P. 104.

# Rye

✔ Lifts mood
✔ Balances blood sugar
✔ Reduces fatigue
✔ Protects against heart disease
✔ Reduces appetite
✔ Lowers the risk of diabetes
✔ Prevents menopausal weight gain
✔ Promotes restful sleep

Rye is rich in fiber and studies have found that eating rye can reduce your daily calorie intake by up to 30 percent. As a whole grain, rye has a calming effect, boosting the production of the feel-good hormone serotonin, promoting restful sleep, and reducing symptoms of depression. It's a fantastic source of antioxidants, too.

**It's rich in ...**

→ Lignans, which promote heart health and improve digestion
→ Fiber, helping to reduce cholesterol levels, promote digestion, ease constipation, and support liver function
→ Magnesium, supporting the nervous system and reducing the risk of diabetes
→ Chromium, which lowers cholesterol and high blood sugar levels, reduces cravings, prevents type-2 diabetes, and lowers the risk of obesity

**Use in ...** delicious sweet and savory rye breads; toast rye bread as croutons for hearty salads; bake in traditional cakes with fruit and honey; use rye berries in salads instead of rice or couscous; serve rye bread or crackers with smoked salmon, egg, tuna, or chicken; use rye berries with herbs and feta to stuff roasted peppers.

SEE: POACHED EGGS & SPINACH, P. 48; TUNA PÂTÉ, P. 61; SWEDISH RYE COOKIES, P. 66; PUMPKIN SOUP, P. 73.

# Pumpkin seeds

✔ Stabilize blood sugar levels
✔ Lift mood
✔ Increase energy
✔ Boost metabolism
✔ Promote restful sleep
✔ Encourage healthy thyroid function
✔ Reduce body fat

Pumpkin seeds contain minerals and amino acids, which aid relaxation and sleep. This is helpful because abdominal fat can be exacerbated by stress. In addition, those who lack good-quality or adequate sleep are more likely to gain weight, partly because the hormones leptin and ghrelin are affected and these influence appetite.

**They are rich in ...**

→ Magnesium, supporting the nervous system and promoting restful sleep
→ Tryptophan, which converts to serotonin to lift mood, relax, and encourage sleep
→ Zinc, which stimulates the pituitary gland to produce thyroid-stimulating hormone (TSH) and boosts metabolism
→ Omega-3 oils, which help to decrease body fat by stimulating the enzymes that transport fat to the parts of the body where it can be burned and used to produce energy

**Use in ...** salads with ricotta cheese; sprinkle on cereals and oatmeal or use in muesli; lightly toast for a blood sugar stabilizing snack; add to muffins or use to top homemade, whole-grain bread; add to fruit crisp toppings or sprinkle over vegetable gratins; stir into risottos.

SEE: SUMMER BERRY GRANOLA, P. 38; TURMERIC-ROASTED PUMPKIN SEEDS, P. 54; PUMPKIN SOUP, P. 73; PUMPKIN, FETA & PINE NUT SALAD, P. 86.

# Carrots

✔ Reduce bloating
✔ Improve liver function
✔ Balance hormones
✔ Ease constipation
✔ Lower cholesterol
✔ Support heart health
✔ Boost immunity
✔ Enhance metabolism

Carrots stimulate and improve liver function, which is partly responsible for hormone balance in the body, as well as improving digestion and to some extent energy levels.

### They are rich in ...

→ Soluble fiber, which lowers blood cholesterol, balances blood sugar, and promotes healthy digestion
→ Beta-carotene, encouraging the health of the heart and liver, boosting immunity, and speeding metabolism
→ Sulfur, a key ingredient of insulin, which converts carbohydrates into energy and supports liver function
→ Vitamin K, good for a healthy nervous system and brain function

**Use in ...** stews, casseroles, and soups; fruit and vegetable juices; roast with thyme and a little olive oil; serve raw with hummus for a satisfying snack; shred and drizzle with lemon vinaigrette for a tasty salad; shred and add to cookies, muffins, and cakes; stir-fry with fresh leafy greens.

SEE: SPICY CARROT & LEMON SOUP, P. 76; SCALLOP, PARSNIP & CARROT SALAD, P. 84; BAKED FISH WITH LEMON GRASS & GREEN PAPAYA SALAD, P. 93; LAMB & APRICOT STEW WITH PEARL BARLEY, P. 100; MOROCCAN CHICKPEAS WITH CARROTS & DATES, P. 104; VEGETABLE & TOFU STIR-FRY, P. 106.

# Apples

✔ Reduce appetite
✔ Support liver function
✔ Boost immunity
✔ Balance blood sugar
✔ Ease constipation
✔ Promote digestion
✔ Provide long-term energy
✔ Support heart function

The carbohydrates in apples are digested slowly, helping to balance blood sugar levels and provide a feeling of fullness. One study found that overweight women who ate the equivalent of three small apples a day lost more weight on a low-calorie diet than women who didn't eat fruit.

**They are rich in ...**

→ Antioxidants that can reduce the absorption of fat, and that help prevent high blood pressure, insulin resistance (a precursor to diabetes), and obesity
→ Pectin, a soluble fiber that supports liver function and healthy digestion, and that balances blood sugar
→ Quercetin, which reduces production of the stress hormone cortisol and supports brain and heart function
→ Polyphenols, which reduce the rate at which sugars are absorbed and stimulate the pancreas to release more insulin

**Use in ...** stuffings for chicken, with seeds, nuts, and whole-wheat bread crumbs; bake in crisps with an oat, cinnamon, and seed topping; add to fruit and vegetable juices; puree and serve with roasted meats.

SEE: APPLE, CINNAMON & ALMOND MUESLI, P. 40; CRANBERRY & APPLE SMOOTHIE, P. 64; CHICKEN & APPLE STEW, P. 97; ALMOND & APPLE CAKE WITH VANILLA YOGURT, P. 113; BAKED APPLES, P. 118.

# Cinnamon

✔ Lowers blood sugar levels
✔ Reduces cravings
✔ Supports liver function
✔ Boosts metabolism
✔ Lowers cholesterol

Studies have found that just half a teaspoon of ground cinnamon a day balances blood sugar levels and reduces cravings. It also helps to reduce levels of the stress hormone cortisol, which can encourage belly fat and slow down metabolism.

**It's rich in ...**

→ MCHP, which enhances the effects of insulin and so lowers blood sugar, reduces some forms of anxiety, and lowers cholesterol
→ Sulfur, which supports the health of the liver and, through that, hormone balance, digestion, and energy levels
→ Calcium, to encourage restful sleep and a healthy nervous system
→ Cinnamaldehyde, helping to balance hormones (in particular, testosterone and progesterone)

**Use in ...** oatmeal; stir into freshly pressed apple juice; add to fruit purees and serve with yogurt with live cultures; add a teaspoon to chicken and lamb casseroles; steep cinnamon sticks in boiling water to make a tea; sprinkle over mashed bananas or applesauce; serve on whole-wheat toast.

SEE: APPLE, CINNAMON & ALMOND MUESLI, P. 40; CHICKEN & APPLE STEW, P. 97; LAMB & APRICOT STEW WITH PEARL BARLEY, P. 100; SLOW-COOKED SPICY BEEF, P. 103; MOROCCAN CHICKPEAS WITH CARROTS & DATES, P. 104; BAKED APPLES, P. 118; SLICED ORANGES WITH ALMONDS, P. 121; CINNAMON BRIOCHE WITH MIXED BERRIES, P. 124.

# Almonds

✔ Promote fat burning
✔ Boost energy levels
✔ Balance blood sugar
✔ Lift mood
✔ Support the liver
✔ Prevent heart disease
✔ Promote relaxation
✔ Support thyroid function
✔ Aid restful sleep

High in fiber and protein, almonds provide a sustained source of energy and help to balance blood sugar levels, which is particularly helpful in dealing with belly fat. Research shows that people who regularly consume almonds have a healthier body weight than those who don't.

**They are rich in ...**
→ Zinc and vitamin $B_{12}$, boosting mood and stimulating the thyroid gland
→ Healthy fats, fighting heart disease and preventing insulin resistance
→ Calcium, magnesium, and tryptophan, encouraging restful sleep and calm
→ Phytoestrogens, balancing hormones

**Use in ...** salads with grapes and goat cheese; spread almond butter on whole-wheat crackers or toast; added to mueslis and granolas, or sprinkle over breakfast cereals; lightly toast and eat as a snack; chop and add to rice salads or as a crunchy topping for carrot or squash soup; use ground almonds in cakes and cookies.

SEE: APPLE, CINNAMON & ALMOND MUESLI, P. 40; BANANA & ALMOND SMOOTHIE, P. 46; CHICKEN & APPLE STEW, P. 97; PUMPKIN CURRY WITH MOROCCAN CHICKPEAS WITH CARROTS & DATES, P. 104; PINK GRAPEFRUIT SALAD, P. 107; ALMOND & APPLE CAKE WITH VANILLA YOGURT, P. 113; SLICED ORANGES WITH ALMONDS, P. 121.

# Eggs

✔ Balance hormones
✔ Support the liver
✔ Boost energy levels
✔ Regulate appetite
✔ Balance blood sugar
✔ Reduce cravings
✔ Encourage thyroid health
✔ Lift mood
✔ Encourage restful sleep

The protein found in eggs contains all eight amino acids necessary for general health and, in particular, the ability to break down food for energy and regeneration. They also contain plenty of the B vitamins, which help to control sugar cravings. Eating eggs for breakfast can reduce daily calorie intake by more than 400 calories. What's more, they contain iodine to support the thyroid gland.

**They are rich in ...**
→ Choline, a soluble mineral that helps prevent fat from being laid down in the liver, thus improving hormone balance
→ Protein, which keeps you fuller for longer, raises energy, and balances sugar levels
→ Vitamin $B_{12}$, helping to metabolize fat
→ Folic acid, lifting mood and supporting the nervous system

**Use in ...** salads and sandwich fillings; frittatas with bell peppers and goat cheese; poach and serve on a bed of wilted spinach; soft-boil and serve with asparagus spears for dipping; use in cakes and baked goods.

SEE: LIGHT CRÊPES, P. 41; DATE & BANANA PANCAKES, P. 42; POACHED EGGS & SPINACH, P. 48; HUEVOS RANCHEROS, P. 50; MOROCCAN BAKED EGGS, P. 52; ASPARAGUS WITH SMOKED SALMON, P. 53; CHILLED GAZPACHO, P. 74; GREEN BEAN & ASPARAGUS SALAD, P. 85, SMOKED HADDOCK WITH POACHED EGGS, P. 92.

# Lentils

✔ Reduce PMS bloating and cravings
✔ Stop abdominal fat being laid down
✔ Balance hormones
✔ Provide sustained energy
✔ Encourage calm
✔ Balance blood sugar
✔ Lift mood
✔ Encourage restful sleep

Rich in protein, lentils help to stabilize blood sugar levels and, through that, reduce belly fat by preventing spikes of insulin that cause your body to lay down excess fat. As natural phytoestrogens, they help to balance hormones and address hormone-related weight gain.

## They are rich in ...

→ Soluble fiber, helping to stabilize blood sugar levels, while providing a steady source of energy
→ Magnesium, which decreases the release of the stress hormone cortisol
→ Protein, providing sustained energy levels, promoting a feeling of fullness, and balancing blood sugar levels
→ Vitamins $B_1$ and $B_2$, easing symptoms of PMS, including bloating, cravings, and mood swings that may lead to comfort eating

**Use in ...** soups, casseroles, stews, and curries; sauté cooked lentils with walnut oil and a little sherry and top with grilled goat cheese; heat and serve cooked lentils with lemon, olive oil, and chives; use in fragrant dahls with paneer cheese; use as a bed for pan-fried scallops.

SEE: BUTTERNUT SQUASH, ROSEMARY & LENTIL SOUP, P. 77; THAI RED VEGETABLE CURRY WITH COCONUT RICE, P. 108.

# Seaweeds

✔ Promote thyroid health
✔ Support the adrenal glands
✔ Balance hormones
✔ Boost energy
✔ Improve metabolism
✔ Reduce risk of heart disease
✔ Regulate blood sugar

All seaweeds, including kelp (kombu and wakame), nori, dulse, arame, and Irish moss, are immensely nutrient-dense sea vegetables with a host of health benefits. With more than 70 minerals and trace elements, and a number of amino acids, they encourage health and well-being. Perhaps most important is their role in supporting glands, such as the thyroid and pituitary, which play an important role in balancing hormones and metabolism.

**They are rich in ...**

→ Iodine, regulating thyroid function and female hormones and encouraging healthy metabolism
→ Iron, boosting energy levels and ease fatigue
→ Phytoestrogens, helping to balance hormones and address hormone-related weight gain
→ Fiber and protein (including 21 amino acids), balancing blood sugar and supporting health on all levels

**Use in ...** sushi; add to quiches or scrambled eggs; sprinkle dried flakes over food instead of salt; add kelp flakes to stews, casseroles, and soups for extra flavor, nutrients, and texture; eat kelp noodles with a light, lemony sauce.

SEE: ROASTED SEAWEED & SESAME SNACK, P. 57; CHICKEN BROCHETTES WITH CUCUMBER & KELP SALAD, P. 94.

# Grapefruit

✔ Boosts metabolism
✔ Balances blood sugar
✔ Supports the liver
✔ Improves digestion
✔ Reduces fat stores
✔ Lowers cholesterol
✔ Eases constipation
✔ Raises energy levels
✔ Lifts mood

Grapefruit is a fiber-rich food that uses up more calories in digestion than it provides, thus helping to reduce fat deposits. It encourages metabolism and helps you to feel full. One study found that people who ate half a grapefruit with every meal for 12 weeks lost an average of 3 lb in weight, while making no other changes to their diet.

**It's rich in ...**

→ Limonoids, which encourage the action of the liver, fight cancer, and lower cholesterol
→ Pectin, good for healthy digestion and blood sugar levels, and for lower cholesterol levels
→ Lycopene (in pink and red grapefruit), protecting the heart and reducing the risk of diabetes
→ Inositol, which promotes the production and release of serotonin, and facilitates the metabolism of fats and cholesterol

**Use in ...** salads with spinach and avocado; top with a little honey and cinnamon and put under the broiler; serve with fresh crab on a bed of arugula; puree a few segments with some mint leaves and crème fraîche for a delicious salad dressing.

SEE: GINGER-BROILED GRAPEFRUIT WITH HONEY YOGURT, P. 44; PUMPKIN CURRY WITH PINK GRAPEFRUIT SALAD, P. 107.

# Black beans

- ✔ Lift mood
- ✔ Encourage sleep
- ✔ Ease symptoms of PMS
- ✔ Raise energy levels
- ✔ Balance blood sugar
- ✔ Reduce appetite and cravings
- ✔ Support healthy digestion
- ✔ Ease constipation
- ✔ Lower cholesterol

Black beans are one of the most nutritious members of the legume family. They are full of antioxidants, protein, and fiber to support health on all levels, and in particular, they encourage optimum digestion and prevent spikes of insulin that can lead to fat deposits.

### They are rich in ...

→ Magnesium, boosting serotonin levels in the brain and encouraging restful sleep

→ Good-quality protein, which stabilizes blood sugar levels, leaves you feeling fuller for longer, and provides energy

→ Soluble fiber, encouraging digestion, reducing the risk of heart disease, and lowering cholesterol

→ Anthocyanins, which lower blood pressure, protect the nervous system and digestive tract, encourage optimum brain function, and balance blood sugar

**Use in ...** burritos served in whole-wheat tortillas with brown rice; use instead of meat or poultry in tacos; stir into soups, stews, and casseroles; serve cold in a salad with corn kernels, chopped bell peppers, avocados, and a zesty lime dressing; use in spicy meat or vegetarian chili.

SEE: BLACK BEAN HUMMUS, P. 60; BLACK BEAN SOUP, P. 70.

# Tuna

✔ Improves heart health
✔ Lifts mood
✔ Supports the thyroid gland
✔ Lowers blood pressure
✔ Beats fatigue
✔ Reduces the impact of stress
✔ Balances blood sugar

Tuna has a host of health-giving properties, many of which address the factors that lead to obesity, such as comfort eating and low mood, poor-quality sleep, inadequate thyroid production, and hormone-related problems such as PMS.

**It's rich in ...**
→ Selenium, which supports thyroid function, lifts moods, and encourages a healthy heart
→ Tyrosine, raising energy levels, helping to deal with stress, producing thyroid hormones, and balancing mood
→ Omega-3 oils, encourageing heart and brain health, reducing symptoms of PMS, and preventing surges in stress hormones that can lead to fat deposits
→ The B vitamins, producing serotonin, promoting restful sleep, and easing the symptoms of PMS and stress

**Use in ...** a traditional salad Niçoise; serve in a lemony sauce with whole-wheat pasta; mix with chopped bell peppers, scallions, chopped tomatoes, and peas in a brown rice salad; mash canned tuna with fat-free Greek yogurt and black beans and serve on toasted rye bread; grill fresh tuna steaks and serve on whole-wheat rolls.

SEE: TUNA PÂTÉ, P. 61; TUNA SKEWERS WITH COCONUT & MANGO SALAD, P. 90.

# Turmeric

✔ Boosts metabolism
✔ Lowers blood sugar
✔ Encourages liver function
✔ Lowers cholesterol
✔ Breaks down fat
✔ Reduces the risk of diabetes
✔ Prevents bloating
✔ Improves digestion

By increasing bile production in the liver, turmeric boosts metabolism and lowers blood pressure, while breaking down fat deposits. It has also been shown to help prevent cancer, reduce bloating, improve digestion, and lower cholesterol.

**It's rich in ...**
→ Curcumin, which lowers cholesterol, boosts metabolism, promotes healthy liver function, and breaks down fats
→ Sulfur, helping to support liver function and balance hormones, prevent heart disease, and improve digestion
→ Iron, which lifts energy levels and banishes fatigue that can be hampering weight-loss efforts
→ Manganese, for a healthy nervous system and energy production
→ Vitamin $B_6$, which works with zinc to help metabolize food into energy

**Use in ...** curries; add to soups and stews; use in relishes; add to omelets; use in rice dishes and with beans.

SEE: TURMERIC-ROASTED PUMPKIN SEEDS, P. 54; BLACK BEAN SOUP, P. 70; PUMPKIN SOUP, P. 73; TUNA SKEWERS WITH COCONUT & MANGO SALAD, P. 90; SLOW-COOKED SPICY BEEF, P. 103; MOROCCAN CHICKPEAS WITH CARROTS & DATES, P. 104; PUMPKIN CURRY WITH PINK GRAPEFRUIT SALAD, P. 107; THAI RED VEGETABLE CURRY, P. 108.

# Dates

✔ Reduce cholesterol
✔ Ease constipation
✔ Boost energy levels
✔ Improve digestion
✔ Lower blood pressure
✔ Balance blood sugar
✔ Boost metabolism
✔ Lift mood
✔ Support restful sleep

Dates have long been used to revitalize and supply energy—for example, when breaking the fast during the month of Ramadan. Rich in fiber, they help to optimize digestion and also prevent constipation. They are rich in tryptophan, good for lifting mood and encouraging regenerative sleep.

**They are rich in ...**

→ Fiber, helping to reduce cholesterol levels, prevent constipation, balance blood sugar levels, and ensure healthy digestion and absorption of nutrients
→ Iron, raising energy levels by improving the oxygen content of your blood
→ Potassium, helping to lower blood pressure, regulate blood sugar levels, and boost immunity
→ The B vitamins (in particular vitamin B$_6$), which help the body metabolize carbohydrates, proteins, and fats, ease symptoms of PMS (including bloating and cravings), promote a healthy nervous system, and maintain healthy blood sugar levels

**Use in ...** lamb and chicken stews; oat bars or cookies; cakes; add to granola or muesli for breakfast; eat whole and fresh as a revitalizing snack.

SEE: DATE & BANANA PANCAKES, P. 42; MOROCCAN CHICKPEAS WITH CARROTS & DATES, P. 104.

# Chicken

✔ Boosts metabolism
✔ Balances blood sugar
✔ Supports the thyroid gland
✔ Aids restful sleep
✔ Lifts mood
✔ Supports the liver

An excellent source of lean, good-quality protein, chicken is ideal for anyone wanting to lose weight. It boosts metabolism and prevents the storage of unwanted fat, while keeping you feeling full for longer.

**It's rich in ...**

→ The B vitamins, which support energy metabolism and production, banishing fatigue and helping to balance mood, energy levels, and blood sugar
→ Selenium, which encourages the action of the thyroid, promotes a healthy immune system, lifts mood, and protects your heart
→ Phosphorus, which is necessary for the healthy functioning of the liver and nervous system
→ Tryptophan, encouraging the release of the feel-good hormone serotonin and promoting restful sleep

**Use in ...** salads with plenty of crunchy vegetables; soups, casseroles, and stews; stuff with apples, walnuts, and whole-wheat bread crumbs and roast whole; stir-fry with Chinese vegetables and chiles; stuff chicken breasts with sun-dried tomatoes, ricotta cheese, and spinach before baking; rub chicken parts with fragrant spices and serve with rice.

SEE: CHICKEN BROCHETTES WITH CUCUMBER & KELP SALAD, P. 94; CHICKEN & BLUEBERRY PASTA SALAD, P. 96; CHICKEN & APPLE STEW, P. 97; ROMAN CHICKEN WITH BELL PEPPERS, P. 98.

# Dark chocolate

✔ Balances blood sugar
✔ Lifts mood
✔ Reduces blood pressure
✔ Eases cravings and addictions
✔ Supports the nervous system
✔ Boosts energy levels
✔ Reduces stress

Dark chocolate is an amazing source of key nutrients, including iron, which boosts energy levels and helps to ensure a good supply of oxygen and nutrients to every cell in your body. Although the stearic acid in dark chocolate is a saturated fat, it does not raise cholesterol levels, but supports the nervous system and produces beneficial hormones.

**It's rich in ...**

→ Theobromine, which enhances physical and mental relaxation
→ Anandamide, which raises levels of serotonin and feel-good chemicals known as endorphins
→ Oleic acid, a cholesterol-busting fat
→ Flavonoids, which help to reduce insulin resistance and stabilize blood sugar levels

**Use in ...** sweet and savory sauces and stews; choose chocolate bars with at least 70 percent cocoa solids and grate onto fresh fruit or yogurt; snack on a handful of chocolate-covered brazil nuts; melt and blend with a banana and yogurt with live cultures for a rich, nutritious smoothie; dip fruit and nuts into a chocolate fondue for a satisfying dessert.

SEE: CHOCOLATE ESPRESSO DESSERTS, P. 110;
CHOCOLATE-DIPPED CHERRIES, P. 112.

# Cheese

✔ Balances blood sugar
✔ Supports thyroid function
✔ Encourages restful sleep
✔ Lifts mood
✔ Aids relaxation
✔ Reduces cravings
✔ Provides relief from PMS
✔ Lowers blood pressure

Cheese is a satisfying, versatile food that is good for weight-loss programs. It helps to reduce cravings for carbohydrates, and it also lifts mood and promotes relaxing sleep. Opt for lower-fat cheeses, such as mozzarella and Edam, when possible.

**It's rich in ...**

➔ Tryptophan, which promotes the release of serotonin, helping you feel uplifted, while banishing cravings
➔ Calcium, which lowers blood pressure, reduces symptoms of PMS, and supports a healthy nervous system
➔ Protein, for balancing blood sugar levels, helping you feel fuller for longer, raising energy levels, and beating belly fat
➔ The B vitamins, in particular vitamin $B_{12}$, which promote energy and the health of the nervous system

**Use in ...** salads with apples, berries, and crispy vegetables; stuff avocado halves with cottage cheese and top with toasted seeds; grate into a warming bowl of soup for extra nutrients; top baked vegetable with grated cheese.

SEE: TUNA PÂTÉ, P. 61; SWEDISH RYE COOKIES, P. 66; PUMPKIN, FETA & PINE NUT SALAD, P. 86; RED PEPPER & FETA ROLLS WITH OLIVES, P. 88; CHICKEN & BLUEBERRY PASTA SALAD, P. 96; CHEESY PORK WITH PARSNIP PUREE, P. 102; BLUEBERRY CHEESECAKE DESSERTS, P. 114.

# Coconut

✔ Regulates thyroid function
✔ Reduces cholesterol
✔ Eases constipation
✔ Raises energy levels
✔ Balances blood sugar
✔ Supports liver function
✔ Increases metabolism
✔ Reduces cravings

While coconut contains saturated fats, these have several health benefits and are easily metabolized by the body to provide long-term, sustainable energy. Coconut contains one of the few fats that can be heated to a high temperature without turning into an unhealthy trans fat.

**It's rich in ...**

➔ Medium-chain triglycerides, a form of saturated fat that regulates thyroid function, improves blood sugar balance, promotes heart health, and metabolizes quickly for sustainable energy
➔ Fiber, reducing cholesterol, aiding digestion, and preventing constipation
➔ Lauric acid, which boosts metabolism and supports immunity
➔ Manganese, good for a healthy nervous system, thyroid function, and energy

**Use in ...** curries and soups, in the form of coconut milk or grated fresh or dried coconut; use dried coconut flakes in muesli and granola; bake dried coconut into oat bars or whole-wheat muffins; grate fresh coconut over sliced mango or serve in a salad with lime and ginger dressing.

SEE: PUMPKIN SOUP, P. 73; TUNA SKEWERS WITH COCONUT & MANGO SALAD, P. 90; PUMPKIN CURRY WITH PINK GRAPEFRUIT SALAD, P. 107; THAI RED VEGETABLE CURRY, P. 108; COCONUT MANGO PUDDING, P. 116.

# WHAT'S YOUR PROBLEM?

It may be that you have tried different diets in the past to no avail, or perhaps you have a health problem that contributes to excess weight. Decide which symptoms affect you and choose from the foods and recipes that can relieve them. There is an icon by each symptom. These icons are used in the recipes to highlight which recipes help combat which symptoms.

## Fat around the middle

Blueberries, tuna, oranges, turkey, sweet potatoes, sunflower seeds, spinach, almonds, kale, eggs, broccoli, green tea, olives, avocado, lentils

**Recipes Include:**
Green tea oatmeal with blueberries, p. 36; Scallop & broccoli broth, p. 68; Tuna skewers with coconut & mango salad, p. 90; Blueberry cheesecake desserts, p. 114.

## Menopausal weight gain

Salmon, tomatoes, barley, lentils, soy products, spinach, oats, watermelon, quinoa, papaya, chickpeas, sardines, pumpkin, brown rice, walnuts, peaches, prunes

**Recipes Include:**
Roasted edamame, p. 56; Raspberry, pineapple & papaya smoothie, p. 65; Butternut squash, rosemary & lentil soup, p. 77; Baked fish with lemon grass & green papaya salad, p. 93.

## Post-pregnancy weight

Salmon, oats, blueberries, lentils, avocado, eggs, broccoli, almonds, oranges, quinoa, kidney beans, yogurt with live cultures, dark chocolate, chicken

**Recipes Include:**
Summer berry granola, p. 38; Green bean & asparagus salad, p. 85; Chicken & apple stew, p. 97; Chocolate espresso desserts, p. 110; Almond & apple cake with vanilla yogurt, p. 113.

## Beer belly

Almonds, eggs, salmon, turkey, quinoa, oats, kale, flaxseeds, walnuts, seaweeds, soy products, blueberries, raspberries, kiwifruit, sweet potatoes, dark chocolate, cheese, lentils

**Recipes Include:**
Roasted edamame, p. 56; Chicken brochettes with cucumber & kelp salad, p. 94; Vegetable & tofu stir-fry, p. 106; Thai red vegetable curry, p. 108.

### Cravings

Apricots, shellfish, peppermint, cheese, mackerel, pumpkin, chickpeas, eggs, dark chocolate, cod, broccoli, Romaine lettuce, cauliflower, tomatoes, endive, cinnamon, apples, pinto beans, oats.
**Recipes Include:**
Apple, cinnamon & almond muesli, p. 40; Peppered beef with salad greens, p. 78; Lamb & apricot stew with pearl barley, p. 100; Moroccan chickpeas with carrots & dates, p. 104.

### Fluctuating blood sugar

Almonds, quinoa, millet, avocado, walnuts, lentils, popcorn, peanuts, oats, apples, sweet potatoes, eggs, grapefruit, pumpkin, raspberries, watermelon, dark chocolate, turmeric, sunflower seeds, cheese, cranberries, tomatoes, pumpkin seeds
**Recipes Include:**
Ginger-broiled grapefruit with honey yogurt, p. 44; Baked apples, p. 118.

### High blood pressure

Celery, tomatoes, flaxseeds, bananas, spinach, mushrooms, butternut squash, seaweeds, papaya, live yogurt, kale, oats, eggs, soy products, tuna, pork, garlic, peanuts, dates, parsnips, scallops
**Recipes Include:**
Poached eggs & spinach, p. 48; Scallop, parsnip & carrot salad, p. 84; Cheesy pork with parsnip puree, p. 102; Thai red vegetable curry with coconut rice, p. 108.

### Stress

Asparagus, beef, milk, almonds, blueberries, tuna, dark chocolate, mango, mushrooms, beets, seaweeds, pumpkin seeds, brown rice, spinach, kiwifruit, chicken
**Recipes Include:**
Turmeric-roasted pumpkin seeds, p. 54; Peppered beef with salad greens, p. 78; Green bean & asparagus salad, p. 85; Coconut mango pudding, p. 116.

## Low mood

Brazil nuts, spinach, oranges, grapefruit, herring, brown rice, spelt, soy products, kidney beans, crab, turkey, green tea, apricots, almonds, lentils, blueberries, dark chocolate, sesame seeds, scallops, kale, pumpkin, eggplant

**Recipes Include:**
Ginger-broiled grapefruit with honey yogurt, p. 44; Eggplant dip with toasted tortillas, p. 62; Pumpkin curry with pink grapefruit salad, p. 107.

## Underactive thyroid

Seaweeds, turkey, dark chocolate, shrimp, beef, oysters, cashew nuts, sunflower seeds, raspberries, eggs, tomatoes, coconut, red bell peppers, brazil nuts, yogurt, chicken, oats, pumpkin seeds

**Recipes Include:**
Raspberry, pineapple & papaya smoothie, p. 65; Red pepper & feta rolls with olives, p. 88; Chicken brochettes with cucumber & kelp salad, p. 94.

## Slow metabolism

Chiles, cherries, blueberries, milk, oats, quinoa, turkey, salmon, coffee, eggs, ginger, garlic, broccoli, almonds, grapefruit, pears, black beans, cider vinegar, turmeric, water, red meat, cinnamon, chicken, split peas, chickpeas

**Recipes Include:**
Turmeric-roasted pumpkin seeds, p. 54; Thai red vegetable curry with coconut rice, p. 108; Cinnamon brioche with mixed berries, p. 124.

## Bloating

Yogurt with live cultures, tuna, rye, asparagus, bananas, ginger, pineapple, papaya, green tea, peppermint, fennel, watercress, melon, salmon, sunflower seeds, almonds, bell peppers, quinoa, cheese, celery

**Recipes Include:**
Date & banana pancakes, p. 42; Banana & almond smoothie, p. 46; Baked fish with lemon grass & green papaya salad, p. 93; Green tea & ginger granita, p. 120.

## Poor digestion

Yogurt with live cultures, black beans, pineapple, papaya, raspberries, artichokes, salmon, ginger, lentils, cider vinegar, bell peppers, brown rice, carrots, sweet potatoes, berries, oats, split peas, apples, rye, cranberries, dates, turmeric, parsnips

**Recipes Include:** Raspberry, pineapple & papaya smoothie, p. 65; Black bean soup, p. 70; Thai red vegetable curry, p. 108.

## Hormone imbalance

Flaxseeds, broccoli, kale, soy products, quinoa, buckwheat, apples, coconut, oranges, turkey, walnuts, green tea, tomatoes, spinach, carrots, eggs, rye, chickpeas, lentils, brown rice, turmeric

**Recipes Include:** Baked tofu sticks, p. 58; Spicy carrot & lemon soup, p. 76; Moroccan chickpeas with carrots & dates, p. 104; Vegetable & tofu stir-fry, p. 106; Green tea & ginger granita, p. 120.

## Constant hunger

Chicken, soy products, eggs, chickpeas, black beans, lentils, rye, whole wheat, dark chocolate, walnuts, almonds, peanuts, yogurt, salmon, popcorn, coconut, cider vinegar, shellfish, pumpkin

**Recipes Include:** Summer berry granola, p. 38; Huevos rancheros, p. 50; Asparagus with smoked salmon, p. 53; Black bean hummus, p. 60; Chocolate espresso desserts, p. 110.

## Low self-esteem

Blueberries, carrots, butternut squash, tomatoes, kale, spinach, Romaine lettuce, alfalfa, rye, cherries, grapes, tuna, salmon, dates, almond, chickpeas, lentils, broccoli

**Recipes Include:** Date & banana pancakes, p. 42; Huevos rancheros, p. 50; Tuna pâté, p. 61; Moroccan chickpeas with carrots & dates, p. 104; Chocolate-dipped cherries, p. 112.

# PUTTING IT
# ALL TOGETHER

| Meal Planner | Monday | Tuesday | Wednesday |
|---|---|---|---|
| Breakfast | Fruity summer milkshake, p. 47 | Summer berry granola, p. 38 | Banana & almond smoothie, p. 46 |
| Morning snack | Turmeric-roasted pumpkin seeds, p. 54 | Cranberry & apple smoothie, p. 64 | Swedish rye cookies, p. 66 |
| Lunch | Scallop & broccoli broth, p. 68 | Black bean soup, p. 70 | Green bean & asparagus salad, p. 85 |
| Afternoon snack | Eggplant dip with toasted tortillas, p. 62 | Tuna pâté, p. 61 | 3 chocolate-covered brazil nuts |
| Dinner | Roman chicken with bell peppers, p. 98 | Lamb & apricot stew with pearl barley, p. 100 | Chicken & blueberry pasta salad, p. 96 |
| Dessert | Chocolate espresso desserts, p. 110 | Cinnamon brioche with mixed berries, p. 124 | Green tea & ginger granita, p. 120 |

# WEEK 1

| Thursday | Friday | Saturday | Sunday |
|---|---|---|---|
| Asparagus with smoked salmon, p. 53 | Green tea oatmeal with blueberries, p. 36 | Light crêpes, p. 41 | Poached eggs & spinach, p. 48 |
| Chocolate-dipped cherries, p. 112 | Black bean hummus, p. 60 | Raspberry, pineapple & papaya smoothie, p. 65 | 5 dried apricots |
| Butternut squash, rosemary & lentil soup, p. 77 | Scallop, parsnip & carrot salad, p. 84 | Chilled gazpacho, p. 74 | Pumpkin, feta & pine nut salad, p. 86 |
| Baked tofu sticks, p. 58 | 1 hard-boiled egg | Roasted seaweed & sesame snack, p. 57 | Roasted edamame beans, p. 56 |
| Tuna skewers with coconut & mango salad, p. 90 | Vegetable & tofu stir-fry, p. 106 | Slow-cooked spicy beef, p. 103 | Chicken brochettes with cucumber & kelp salad, p. 94 |
| Almond & apple cake with vanilla yogurt, p. 113 | Blueberry cheesecake desserts, p. 114 | Coconut mango pudding, p. 116 | Sliced oranges with almonds, p. 121 |

| Meal Planner | Monday | Tuesday | Wednesday |
|---|---|---|---|
| **Breakfast** | Apple, cinnamon & almond muesli, p. 40 | Asparagus with smoked salmon, p. 53 | Poached eggs & spinach, p. 48 |
| **Morning snack** | 1 hard-boiled egg | Turmeric-roasted pumpkin seeds, p. 54 | Cottage cheese and sliced avocado on a rye crispbread |
| **Lunch** | Sushi rice salad, p. 80 | Pumpkin soup, p. 73 | Spicy carrot & lemon soup, p. 76 |
| **Afternoon snack** | Eggplant dip with toasted tortillas, p. 62 | Swedish rye cookies, p. 66 | Cranberry & apple smoothie, p. 64 |
| **Dinner** | Cheesy pork with parsnip puree, p. 102 | Chicken & apple stew, p. 97 | Thai red vegetable curry with coconut rice, p. 108 |
| **Dessert** | Grilled peaches & apricots with honey yogurt, p. 122 | Chocolate-dipped cherries, p. 112 | Sliced oranges with almonds, p. 121 |

# WEEK 2

| Thursday | Friday | Saturday | Sunday |
|---|---|---|---|
| Ginger-broiled grapefruit with honey yogurt, p. 44 | Huevos rancheros, p. 50 | Date & banana pancakes, p. 42 | Moroccan baked eggs, p. 52 |
| Baked tofu sticks, p. 58 | Roasted edamame, p. 56 | Raspberry, pineapple & papaya smoothie, p. 65 | Black bean hummus, p. 60 |
| Lettuce wrappers with crab, p. 82 | Split pea & parsnip soup, p. 72 | Peppered beef with salad greens, p. 78 | Red pepper & feta rolls with olives, p. 88 |
| 5 dried apricots | Tuna pâté, p. 61 | Roasted seaweed & sesame snack, p. 57 | 3 chocolate-covered brazil nuts |
| Smoked haddock with poached eggs, p. 92 | Baked fish with lemon grass & green papaya salad, p. 93 | Moroccan chickpeas with carrots & dates, p. 104 | Pumpkin curry with pink grapefruit salad, p. 107 |
| Coconut mango pudding, p. 116 | Baked apples, p. 118 | Chocolate espresso desserts, p. 110 | Green tea & ginger granita, p. 120 |

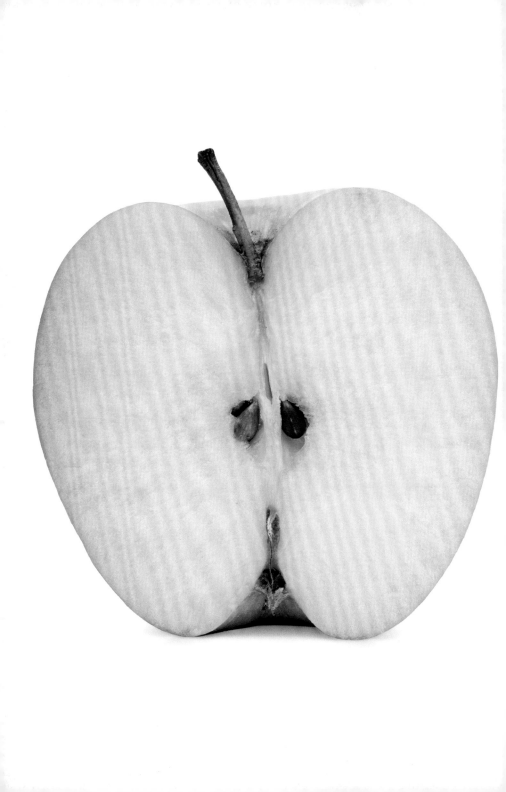

# THIN
## RECIPES

# GREEN TEA OATMEAL WITH BLUEBERRIES

An ingenious way to reap the health benefits of green tea, alongside fat-busting blueberries and deliciously soothing oats.

**Preparation time:** 5 minutes, plus steeping
**Cooking time:** 10 minutes
**Serves 4**
................

5 cups **water**
4 **green tea bags**
2¼ cups **rolled oats**
⅔ cup **blueberries**
2 tablespoons **low-fat Greek yogurt with live cultures**
2 tablespoons **skim milk**
2 tablespoons **maple syrup**

Place the measured water in a large saucepan, bring to a boil, and add the tea bags. Remove from the heat and let steep for 5 minutes.

......................................

Remove the tea bags and return to the heat. Stir in the rolled oats and return to a boil. Reduce the heat and simmer for 4–5 minutes, stirring frequently.

.................................................................

Add the blueberries and continue to cook for another 2–3 minutes, or until the blueberries are warmed through and just starting to burst. Remove from the heat and divide among 4 serving bowls.

.................................................................

Thin the yogurt with the skim milk and pour over the oatmeal. Drizzle over the maple syrup and serve immediately.

.................................................................

# SUMMER BERRY GRANOLA

Serve this satisfying, energy-boosting granola with milk, yogurt, and the berries of your choice.

**Preparation time:** 10 minutes
**Cooking time:** 10 minutes
**Serves 4**
··············

olive oil spray
2¼ cups **rolled oats**
3 tablespoons **pumpkin seeds**
⅔ cup **mixed nuts**, toasted
  and coarsely chopped
1 tablespoon **maple syrup**,
  plus extra to serve
1¼ cups **skim milk**
1½ cups **mixed summer berries**,
  including **blueberries** and **raspberries**
**low-fat Greek yogurt with live cultures**,
  to serve

Spray a baking sheet lightly with oil. Put the oats, seeds, and nuts in a bowl and stir in the maple syrup. Spread the mixture out on the prepared baking sheet and place in a preheated oven, at 350°F, for 5 minutes.

·······················

Remove from the oven and stir well. Return to the oven and cook for another 3–4 minutes, until lightly toasted. Let cool.

·······························

Divide the granola among 4 serving bowls and pour over the milk. Top with the berries and serve with yogurt and a drizzle of maple syrup.

···········································

Any leftover granola can be stored in an airtight container for up to a week.
·······················································

# APPLE, CINNAMON & ALMOND MUESLI

Prepare this the evening before and refrigerate overnight for an instant energy-boosting breakfast, full of fat-busting nutrients.

**Preparation time:** 10 minutes, plus chilling
**Cooking time:** 5 minutes (optional)
**Serves 4**
...............

2 cups **rolled oats**
1 cup **vanilla-flavored soy milk**
1 cup **almond milk**
3 **red apples**, washed, cored, and chopped
⅓ cup **almonds**, crushed
3 tablespoons **honey**
1 teaspoon **ground cinnamon**

Put the oats and milks into a bowl, stir well, and let stand for a few minutes. Stir in the apples, almonds, honey, and cinnamon, cover, and refrigerate overnight.

...........................................................

Serve cold, or warm gently in a saucepan or a microwave oven before serving.

...........................................................

# LIGHT CRÊPES

Top these delicious French-style crêpes with any fruit compote or fresh fruit. Sprinkle with cinnamon, sesame seeds, or nuts.

**Preparation time:** 10 minutes, plus standing
**Cooking time:** about 20 minutes
**Serves 4**
··············

1 cup **whole-wheat flour**
1 **egg**
1¼ cups **skim milk**
1 teaspoon **vegetable oil**, plus
 extra for greasing

**To serve**
**apple compote**
**ground cinnamon**
**cottage cheese**

Sift the flour into a mixing bowl, then tip the bran in the sifter into the bowl. Beat the egg with the milk and oil, then slowly add to the flour, stirring constantly to form a smooth batter. Let stand for about 20 minutes, then stir again.

··············································

Heat a nonstick skillet over medium heat, then grease the skillet with a little oil on a piece of paper towel. When the skillet is hot, add 2 tablespoons of the crêpe batter and shake the pan so that it spreads.

··········································································

Cook the crêpe for about 2 minutes, until the underside is lightly browned, then flip or turn over and cook the other side for a minute or so.

··························

Transfer to a plate and keep warm in a low oven while you cook the remaining crêpes, stacking them one on top of the other as they are cooked. The batter, which should be like runny pancake batter, should make 8 crêpes in all.

··························

Top the crêpes with apple compote, a sprinkling of cinnamon, and a spoonful of cottage cheese, roll up, and serve immediately.

··························

# DATE & BANANA PANCAKES

These fluffy pancakes can be made the night before and reheated in the oven wrapped in aluminum foil.

**Preparation time:** 15 minutes
**Cooking time:** 20 minutes
**Serves 4**

¾ cup pitted and finely chopped **dried dates**
⅔ cup boiling **water**
⅔ cup **whole-wheat** or **buckwheat flour**
⅔ cup **all-purpose flour**
1 teaspoon **baking powder**
½ teaspoons **salt**
1 teaspoon **ground cinnamon**
2 tablespoons **sugar**
1 extra-large **egg**
⅔ cup **skim milk**
2 tablespoons **olive oil**
2 tablespoons **coconut oil**

**To serve**
2 ripe **bananas**, thinly sliced
**maple syrup**

Put the dates into a small bowl with the measured boiling water and set aside to soak.

Meanwhile, put the flours into a mixing bowl with the baking powder, salt, cinnamon, and sugar. Beat the egg with the milk and olive oil, then slowly add to the flour mixture, stirring constantly to form a smooth batter. Drain any excess liquid from the dates and stir into the pancake batter.

Heat a nonstick skillet over medium heat and add a little coconut oil. When it starts to sizzle, pour in a little pancake batter. Cook for about 2 minutes, until bubbles begin to appear on the surface, then carefully turn over with a spatula and cook the other side for another minute.

Transfer to a plate and keep warm in a low oven while you cook the remaining pancakes. Divide among warm serving plates, top with sliced bananas, and drizzle with maple syrup.

# GINGER-BROILED GRAPEFRUIT WITH HONEY YOGURT

A warming, healthy way to start the day, this fragrant grapefruit will jump-start the metabolism and lift the mood.

**Preparation time:** 5 minutes
**Cooking time:** 5 minutes
**Serves 4**
................

½ inch piece of fresh **ginger root**, peeled and finely grated
2 tablespoons packed **brown sugar**
3 tablespoons **honey**
2 **red** or **pink grapefruits**, halved horizontally
½ cup **low-fat Greek yogurt with live cultures**

Put the ginger and brown sugar into a small bowl, add 1 teaspoon of the honey, and mix to a paste. Arrange the grapefruit halves on a broiler pan, cut side up, and spread with the ginger paste.

....................................................

Place under a preheated hot broiler for 5 minutes, or until lightly browned and bubbling. Meanwhile, mix together the yogurt and remaining honey.

....................................................

Serve the hot grapefruit immediately, with the honeyed yogurt on the side.

....................................................

# BANANA & ALMOND SMOOTHIE

Nourishing almond milk provides extra nutrients and protein in this filling smoothie, perfect for a sustaining breakfast.

**Preparation time:** 5 minutes
**Serves 4**
................

1⅓ cups **almond milk**
2 **bananas**, peeled and chopped
½ teaspoons **ground cinnamon**
½ teaspoons **vanilla extract**
6 **ice cubes**

Put all the ingredients into a blender or food processor and blend until smooth. Pour into tall glasses and serve immediately.
...............................................................

# FRUITY SUMMER MILK SHAKE

This is the perfect breakfast for a busy morning, but also makes a good evening snack if you struggle to sleep.

**Preparation time:** 5 minutes
**Serves 4**
................

2 ripe **peaches**, halved, pitted, and chopped
2 cups halved or quartered, hulled **strawberries**
2½ cups **raspberries**
1¾ cups **skim milk**
**ice cubes**, to serve

Put the fruit into a blender or food processor and blend until smooth, scraping the mixture down from the sides of the bowl, if necessary.
.................................................

Add the milk and blend again until the mixture is smooth and frothy. Pour the milk shake over ice cubes in tall glasses and serve immediately.
.................................................

# POACHED EGGS & SPINACH

Eggs are an excellent way to start the day, making sure you eat fewer calories and feel satisfied for longer.

**Preparation time:** 5 minutes
**Cooking time:** 10 minutes
**Serves 4**

················

24 **cherry tomatoes** on the vine
2 tablespoons **balsamic glaze**
small bunch of **basil**, leaves removed
4 extra-large **eggs**
3½ cups **baby spinach**
**sea salt** and **black pepper**
4 thick slices of **rye bread**, toasted, to serve

Lay the cherry tomato vines in an ovenproof dish, drizzle with the balsamic glaze, sprinkle with the basil leaves, and season to taste. Put into a preheated oven, at 350°F, for 8–10 minutes or until the tomatoes begin to collapse.

Meanwhile, bring a large saucepan of water to a gentle simmer. Carefully break 2 eggs into the water and cook for 3 minutes, until the whites are just set. Remove with a slotted spoon and keep warm while cooking the remaining eggs.

Arrange the spinach on 4 serving plates and top each plate with a poached egg. Transfer the tomatoes to the plates and drizzle with any cooking juices. Serve immediately with the rye toast, cut into strips for dipping.

# HUEVOS RANCHEROS

This twist on a Mexican classic takes just half an hour to cook and contains chromium-rich onions and tomatoes to balance blood sugar.

**Preparation time:** 15 minutes
**Cooking time:** 30 minutes
**Serves 4**
................

1 tablespoon **olive oil**
2 **onions**, finely chopped
2 **red bell peppers**, cored, seeded, and finely chopped
4 **garlic cloves**, finely chopped
1 (28 oz) can **diced tomatoes**
1 teaspoon chopped **oregano**
½ teaspoons **ground cumin**
1 **red chile**, seeded and finely chopped
1 tablespoon **cider vinegar**
1 cup rinsed and drained canned **black beans**
4 **eggs**
2 tablespoons chopped fresh **cilantro**
**sea salt** and **black pepper**
soft **whole-wheat tortillas**, warmed, to serve

Heat the oil in a large saucepan over medium heat, add the onions, and sauté for 5 minutes, or until softened. Add the bell peppers and garlic and sauté for another 5 minutes.

....................................

Stir in the tomatoes, oregano, cumin, chile, and vinegar and bring to a boil. Reduce the heat and simmer gently for 10 minutes.

....................................

Season to taste and stir in the beans. When the beans have warmed through, make 4 holes in the tomato mixture and crack an egg into each. Cover the pan and cook for 5 minutes, until the eggs have set.

....................................

Sprinkle with the cilantro and serve immediately with warm tortillas.

....................................

# MOROCCAN BAKED EGGS

Perfect for brunch or a late, lazy breakfast, these gorgeous baked eggs will satisfy even the biggest appetite.

**Preparation time:** 10 minutes
**Cooking time:** 25–30 minutes
**Serves 4**
················

1 tablespoon **olive oil**
1 **onion**, chopped
2 **garlic cloves**, sliced
1 teaspoon **ras el hanout spice mix**
¼ teaspoons **ground cinnamon**
1 teaspoon **ground coriander**
1 (28 oz) can **cherry tomatoes**
    or **diced tomatoes**
¼ cup chopped fresh **cilantro**
4 **eggs**
**sea salt** and **black pepper**
**crusty bread**, to serve

Heat the olive oil in a skillet over medium heat, add the onion and garlic, and sauté for 6–7 minutes or until softened and lightly golden, stirring occasionally.

Stir in the spices and cook for another minute, then add the tomatoes. Season generously and simmer gently for 8–10 minutes. Stir in 3 tablespoons of the cilantro.

Divide the tomato mixture among 4 ramekins or other individual ovenproof dishes, then crack an egg into each dish. Place in a preheated oven, 400°F, for 8–10 minutes, until the egg whites are just set. Cook for another 2–3 minutes if you prefer the eggs to be cooked through.

Serve sprinkled with the remaining cilantro and plenty of crusty bread on the side.

# ASPARAGUS WITH SMOKED SALMON

This surprisingly low-calorie breakfast will help to reduce bloating, lift the mood, and boost energy levels.

**Preparation time:** 10 minutes
**Cooking time:** 5–10 minutes
**Serves 4**

8 oz **asparagus spears**, trimmed
3 tablespoons coarsely chopped **hazelnuts**
4 teaspoons **olive oil**
¼ cup **lime juice**
1 teaspoon **Dijon mustard**
8 **quail eggs**
8 oz **smoked salmon**
**sea salt** and **black pepper**

Cook the asparagus spears in a steamer set over a saucepan of gently simmering water for 5 minutes, until just tender.

Meanwhile, place the nuts on an aluminum foil-lined broiler pan and place under a preheated medium broiler until lightly browned. Put the oil, lime juice, and mustard into a small bowl, season to taste, and stir in the hot nuts. Set aside and keep warm.

Lower the eggs into a small saucepan of gently simmering water using a slotted spoon and cook for 1 minute. Remove from the heat and let stand for 1 minute, then drain the eggs, rinse in cold water, and drain again.

Tear the salmon into strips and divide it among 4 serving plates, folding and twisting the strips attractively. Arrange the asparagus on the plates with the salmon.

Peel and halve the eggs and arrange on top of the salmon and asparagus. Drizzle with the warm nut dressing and serve sprinkled with a little black pepper.

# TURMERIC-ROASTED PUMPKIN SEEDS

Great for thyroid function and attacking body fat, pumpkin seeds make an ideal snack at any time of day.

**Preparation time:** 10 minutes, plus cooling
**Cooking time:** 15–20 minutes
**Serves 4**
·············

1 cup **pumpkin seeds**
½ teaspoon **sea salt**
1 teaspoon **ground turmeric**
1 teaspoon **ground cumin**
1 tablespoon **olive oil**

Put all the ingredients into a large bowl and toss until well coated, then spread out in an even layer on a baking sheet lined with parchment paper.

····················································

Place in a preheated oven, at 275°F, for 15–20 minutes, or until the seeds are golden and beginning to pop. Let cool on the baking sheet before serving.

··························································································

# ROASTED EDAMAME

This is a great way to serve fiber-rich, hormone-balancing edamame (soybeans). Use fresh or frozen beans.

**Preparation time:** 10 minutes
**Cooking time:** 15 minutes
**Serves 4**
................

2 teaspoons **olive oil**
¼ teaspoon **dried basil**
½ teaspoon **chili powder**
½ teaspoon **ground cumin**
¼ teaspoon **paprika**
½ teaspoon **black pepper**
1⅔ cup shelled **edamame (soybeans)**,
    defrosted if frozen

Put the oil, herbs, and spices into a large bowl and use the back of a spoon to work into a smooth powder. Add the edamame and toss well to coat.
..................................

Spread out the beans on a baking sheet lined with parchment paper and place in a preheated oven, at 375°F, for about 15 minutes, stirring once, until the beans begin to brown and smell fragrant.
..................................

Serve the edamame warm or cold. Store any leftover beans in an airtight container.
..................................

# ROASTED SEAWEED & SESAME SNACK

This is a good way to get thyroid-supporting seaweed into the diet. Use the sheets of nori seaweed that are used to wrap sushi.

**Preparation time:** 10 minutes, plus marinating
**Cooking time:** 20 minutes
**Serves 4-6**

......................

1 tablespoon **olive oil**
1 tablespoon **sesame oil**
1 teaspoon **lime juice**
½ teaspoons **sea salt**
8 sheets of **nori seaweed**

Put the olive oil, sesame oil, lime juice, and salt into a small bowl and mix well. Lay a sheet of nori on a board and brush lightly with the oil mix.

......................................

Place a second sheet on top and repeat, then continue until all 8 sheets have been brushed with oil. Roll up the stack of nori and wrap tightly in plastic wrap. Let marinate for 30-45 minutes.

...............................................

Heat a nonstick skillet over medium heat. Place a sheet of nori in the pan and cook for about 1 minute, then turn over and cook the other side until the seaweed is crisp and toasted.

...............................

Transfer the toasted nori to a plate and repeat with the remaining sheets, stacking them one on top of the other on the plate as they are toasted.

...............................

Cut the stack into squares with a sharp knife, then separate the layers. Serve warm or cold.

......................

# BAKED TOFU STICKS

Serve these delicious snacks hot or cold to provide a hit of calming calcium and good-quality protein to keep you going through the day.

**Preparation time:** 10 minutes, plus marinating
**Cooking time:** 30 minutes
**Makes 24**
·················

12 oz firm **tofu**
¼ cup **light soy sauce**, plus extra to serve
⅔ cup **water**
1 inch piece of fresh **ginger root**, peeled and finely grated
3 **garlic cloves**, finely chopped
2 tablespoons **sesame oil**
**oil**, for greasing
2 tablespoons **sesame seeds**

Cut the tofu into 24 sticks and put into a shallow dish. Put the soy sauce, measured water, ginger, garlic, and sesame oil into a small bowl and whisk to combine. Pour the marinade over the tofu, covering it evenly, then let marinate for 30 minutes, turning once.

·······················

Transfer the sticks to a lightly greased baking sheet and sprinkle with the sesame seeds. Place in a preheated oven, at 425°F, for 15 minutes, basting with any remaining marinade if they look dry.

·······························································

Turn the baking sheet and cook for another 15 minutes, or until all of the liquid has been absorbed and the sticks are golden brown. Serve hot or cold with a little extra soy sauce for dipping.
·······························································

# BLACK BEAN HUMMUS

This delicious hummus takes only minutes to prepare and provides a good boost of the B vitamins.

**Preparation time:** 5 minutes
**Serves 4-6**
......................

1 (15 oz) can **black beans,**
   rinsed and drained
finely grated zest and juice of 1 **lemon**
2 tablespoons **tahini**
2 **garlic cloves**
1 teaspoon **ground cumin**
½ teaspoon **black pepper**
½ teaspoon **cayenne pepper**
½ teaspoon **paprika**, plus extra to garnish
12 **black ripe olives** in liquid, pitted,
   plus 2 tablespoons of the liquid
**carrot sticks**, to serve

Put the beans into a blender or food processor, reserving a few for garnish. Add the remaining ingredients and blend until smooth.

....................................

Transfer to a serving bowl, top with the reserved beans, and sprinkle with paprika. Serve with carrot sticks for dipping.

..................................................................

# TUNA PÂTÉ

Rich in omega-3 oils to support heart health and beat fatigue, tuna makes the perfect pick-me-up snack.

**Preparation time:** 10 minutes, plus chilling
**Serves 4**
................

1 (5 oz) can **tuna** in spring water
½ cup **reduced-fat cream cheese**
1 **scallion**, finely chopped
finely grated zest and juice of 1 **lemon**
**sea salt** and **black pepper**
**rye crackers**, to serve

Put all the ingredients into a blender or food processor and pulse until almost smooth, but still with a little texture.
.........................................................

Transfer to a serving bowl and chill in the refrigerator for 20–30 minutes. Serve with rye crackers.
.............................................

# EGGPLANT DIP WITH TOASTED TORTILLAS

For extra flavor and nutrition, you could brush your tortillas with a little olive oil and sprinkle with sesame seeds before toasting.

**Preparation time:** 15 minutes, plus cooling
**Cooking time:** 10–15 minutes
**Serves 4**
················

¼ cup **olive oil**
1 teaspoon **ground cumin**
1 large **eggplant**, cut into ¼ inch-thick slices
⅔ cup **low-fat Greek yogurt**
   **with live cultures**
1 small **garlic clove**, crushed
2 tablespoons chopped fresh **cilantro**
1 tablespoon **lemon juice**
4 soft **whole-wheat tortillas**
**sea salt** and **black pepper**

Mix three-quarters of the oil with the cumin, season to taste, and brush all over the eggplant slices. Cook in a preheated ridged grill pan or under a preheated hot broiler for 3–4 minutes on each side until charred and tender. Let cool.

Chop the eggplant finely and put into a bowl with the yogurt, garlic, cilantro, lemon juice, and the remaining oil. Mix well, season to taste, and transfer to a serving bowl.

Place the tortillas under a preheated hot broiler for 1–2 minutes on each side, until lightly toasted. Cut into triangles and serve immediately with the eggplant dip.

# CRANBERRY & APPLE SMOOTHIE

Cranberries are all-round superfoods, boosting energy, balancing blood sugar, aiding digestion, promoting heart health, and boosting immunity.

**Preparation time:** 10 minutes
**Serves 4**
...............

6 **crisp, sweet apples**
2 cups frozen **cranberries**
1 tablespoon **cider vinegar**
1¾ cups **low-fat plain yogurt**
    **with live cultures**
⅓ cup **honey**
**ice cubes**, to serve (optional)

Rinse the apples and chop them coarsely, without removing the skin and cores. Juice the apple chunks in an electric juicer, or put into a blender or food processor and blend until smooth, then pass the juice through a fine strainer.

Transfer the apple juice to a blender or food processor, add the cranberries, vinegar, yogurt, and honey, and process briefly.

Pour the smoothie into tall glasses, add ice cubes, if using, and serve immediately.

# RASPBERRY, PINEAPPLE & PAPAYA SMOOTHIE

This smoothie is guaranteed to nudge the digestive system and metabolism into action.

**Preparation time:** 10 minutes
**Serves 4**
................

1 **pineapple**, peeled and cut into chunks
1 large **papaya**, peeled, seeded,
   and cut into chunks
1 cup fresh or frozen **raspberries**
½ cup **orange juice**
1 tablespoon chopped **mint**
10 **ice cubes** (optional)

Put all the ingredients, with the ice cubes, if using, into a blender or food processor and blend until smooth. Serve immediately in tall glasses.

.........................................................

# SWEDISH RYE COOKIES

These crunchy cookies are rich in blood sugar-balancing whole grains and make an excellent snack or even a light dessert.

**Preparation time:** 20 minutes, plus chilling
**Cooking time:** 6–7 minutes
**Makes 24**
··················

¾ cup **rye flour**
¾ cup **whole-wheat flour**
½ teaspoon **sea salt**
½ cup **light cream cheese**
1 stick **unsalted butter**, softened
½ cup **superfine** or **granulated sugar**,
    plus extra for dusting

Put the flours and salt into a mixing bowl, stir well to mix, then set aside. Put the cream cheese and butter into a separate bowl and beat with a handheld electric mixer until fluffy.

Add the sugar and continue beating until it has all been incorporated. Stir in the flour mixture until just combined.

Turn out the dough onto a lightly floured surface and knead it briefly. Shape into a ball, wrap in plastic wrap, and chill in the refrigerator for 15 minutes, until firm.

Roll out the dough on a lightly floured surface to about ¼ inch thick. Use a 2½ inch cookie cutter or the top of a glass to cut out 24 cookies, rerolling the scraps as required.

Arrange the cookies on 2 baking sheets lined with parchment paper and place in a preheated oven, at 350°F, for 6–7 minutes, until turning golden at the edges. Dust with the sugar and let cool on the baking sheets.

Store the cookies in an airtight container for up to a week.

# SCALLOP & BROCCOLI BROTH

Shellfish is a wonderful source of zinc, which helps to control appetite and encourage weight loss.

**Preparation time:** 10 minutes, plus steeping
**Cooking time:** 25 minutes
**Serves 4**

5 cups **vegetable** or **chicken stock**
¾ inch piece of fresh **ginger root**, peeled and cut into matchsticks, peel reserved
1 tablespoon **dark soy sauce**
3 **scallions**, finely sliced
1 small **broccoli**, cut into small florets
1 small **red chile**, seeded and finely sliced (optional)
12 large **scallops** with roes
a few drops of **Thai fish sauce**
2 tablespoons **lime juice**
**sesame oil**, to serve

Put the stock into a large saucepan over high heat with the ginger peel and boil for 15 minutes. Set aside and let steep for another 15 minutes.

Strain the stock into a clean saucepan, add the remaining ginger, the soy sauce, scallions, broccoli, and chile, if using, and simmer for 5 minutes.

Add the scallops and simmer for another 3 minutes or until just cooked through. Season with Thai fish sauce and lime juice and serve immediately with a few drops of sesame oil.

# BLACK BEAN SOUP

Black beans are incredibly nutritious, providing a host of the B vitamins, antioxidants, and fiber to balance blood sugar.

**Preparation time:** 15 minutes
**Cooking time:** 30 minutes
**Serves 4**

................

1 tablespoon **olive oil**
1 large **onion**, chopped
2 teaspoons **cumin seeds**
1 inch piece of fresh **ginger root**,
     peeled and grated
4 **garlic cloves**, finely chopped
1 large **tomato**, chopped
2 tablespoons **tomato paste**
2 teaspoons **ground turmeric**
2½ cups **vegetable stock**
2 (15 oz) cans **black beans**,
     rinsed and drained
**sea salt** and **black pepper**

**To serve**
handful of fresh **cilantro**, chopped
¼ cup **low-fat crème fraîche** or **plain yogurt**

Heat the oil in a large saucepan over medium heat, add the onion, and cook for 5 minutes, until softened. Add the cumin seeds and cook for another 2–3 minutes.

Stir in the ginger, garlic, and tomato and continue to cook, stirring frequently, until the tomato begins to break down. Add the tomato paste, turmeric, stock, and half the beans and cook for another 10 minutes.

Season to taste, put into a blender or food processor, in batches if necessary, and blend until smooth. Return to the pan, stir in the remaining beans and heat through. Transfer to warm bowls and serve with a swirl of crème fraîche and a sprinkling of cilantro.

# SPLIT PEA & PARSNIP SOUP

Chock-full of protein, fiber, and the B vitamins, this warming soup has a tasty pat of cilantro butter on top as a treat.

**Preparation time:** 20 minutes, plus soaking
**Cooking time:** 1¼ hours
**Serves 4**
...............

1 cup **yellow split peas**,
   soaked overnight in cold water
2 unpeeled **parsnips**, cut into chunks
1 **onion**, coarsely chopped
6 cups **chicken** or **vegetable stock**
**sea salt** and **black pepper**
toasted **whole-wheat pita breads**, to serve

**Cilantro butter**
1 teaspoon **cumin seeds**, coarsely crushed
1 teaspoon **coriander seeds**, coarsely
   crushed
1 **garlic clove**, finely chopped
4 tablespoons **butter**, softened
small bunch of fresh **cilantro**,
   finely chopped

Drain the soaked split peas and put into a saucepan with the parsnips, onion, and stock. Bring to a boil and cook for 10 minutes. Reduce the heat, cover, and simmer for 1 hour or until the split peas are soft.
........................

Meanwhile, make the cilantro butter by dry-frying the cumin and coriander seeds and garlic in a small saucepan until lightly toasted. Mix into the butter with the chopped cilantro and season to taste. Place on a piece of aluminum foil, shape into a log, wrap tightly, and chill in the refrigerator until needed.
.............................................

Coarsely mash the soup with a potato masher, or put, in batches, into a blender or food processor and blend until smooth, if preferred. Reheat and stir in half the cilantro butter until melted.
.............................................

Add a little water if the soup is too thick, then season to taste. Ladle into warm bowls and top each bowl with a slice of the cilantro butter. Serve with toasted whole-wheat pita breads.
.............................

# PUMPKIN SOUP

These spices make this antioxidant-rich soup ideal for a weight-loss program. Try it cold in the summer months.

**Preparation time:** 20 minutes
**Cooking time:** 20 minutes
**Serves 4**
................

2 tablespoons **olive oil**
1 teaspoon **cumin seeds**
1 teaspoon **ground turmeric**
1 teaspoon **ground coriander**
1 teaspoon **ground cinnamon**
2 small **red onions**, diced
2 **celery sticks**, chopped
1 inch piece of fresh **ginger root**,
    peeled and grated
1 **red chile**, seeded and finely sliced
3 **garlic cloves**, finely sliced
finely grated zest and juice of 2 **limes**
8 cups, peeled, seeded, and diced **pumpkin**
    or **butternut squash**
2½ cups **vegetable stock**
1¾ cups **coconut milk**
25 g (1 oz) fresh **cilantro**, chopped,
    plus extra to serve
**sea salt** and **black pepper**

**To serve**
2 tablespoons grated fresh or dried **coconut**
2 tablespoons **pumpkin seeds**
toasted **rye bread**

Heat the olive oil in a large saucepan over medium heat, add the cumin, turmeric, ground coriander, and cinnamon and cook for 1 minute.
........................

Add the onion, celery, ginger, chile, and garlic and cook for another 4–5 minutes, then stir in the lime zest, pumpkin, and stock. Bring to a boil, then reduce the heat, cover, and simmer for about 8 minutes, or until the pumpkin is beginning to soften.
..............................................

Stir in the coconut milk and continue to cook until the pumpkin starts to break up. Add the fresh cilantro and the lime juice and remove from the heat.
.......................................

Put the soup into a blender or food processor, in batches if necessary, and blend until smooth. Return to the pan, season to taste, and heat through. Serve in warm bowls, sprinkled with fresh cilantro, grated coconut, and pumpkin seeds, with toasted rye bread.
.............................

# CHILLED GAZPACHO

This cold soup is surprisingly filling, and the chopped egg will provide energy to see you through the afternoon.

**Preparation time:** 20 minutes, plus chilling
**Serves 4**
................

5 ripe **tomatoes**
½ **cucumber**, coarsely chopped
2 **red bell peppers**, cored, seeded,
   and coarsely chopped
1 **celery stick**, chopped
2 **garlic cloves**, peeled
½ **red chile**, seeded and sliced
small handful of fresh **cilantro**
   or **flat leaf parsley**, plus extra to serve
2 tablespoons **cider vinegar**
2 tablespoons **tomato paste**
¼ cup **olive oil**
**sea salt**

**To serve**
**ice cubes**
2 hard-boiled **eggs**, finely chopped
finely chopped **cucumber**,
   **green bell pepper** and **onion**
8 **blinis** (optional)

Put the tomatoes into a bowl and pour over enough boiling water to cover. Let stand for 1–2 minutes, then drain, cut a cross at the stem end of each tomato, and peel off the skins.

......................

Coarsely chop the tomato flesh and mix with the cucumber, red bell peppers, celery, garlic, chile, and cilantro or parsley. Stir in the vinegar, tomato paste, and oil and season with salt.

.............................

Put the mixture into a blender or food processor, in batches if necessary, and blend until smooth. Taste and add more salt if necessary, then chill in the refrigerator for up to 24 hours until ready to serve.

...................................................................

Serve the soup in large bowls, sprinkled with ice cubes and chopped cilantro or parsley. Put the chopped egg, cucumber, green bell pepper, and onion into separate bowls and serve on the side with the blinis, if desired.
...................

# SPICY CARROT & LEMON SOUP

Warming, relaxing ginger, refreshing lemon and blood sugar-balancing carrot come together in this delicious, satisfying soup.

**Preparation time:** 10 minutes
**Cooking time:** 30 minutes
**Serves 4**
...............

2 tablespoons **olive oil**
2 large **onions**, chopped
1 inch piece of **fresh ginger root**,
    peeled and finely grated
3 **garlic cloves**, finely chopped
10 unpeeled **carrots**, sliced
2 unpeeled **parsnips**, sliced
finely grated zest and juice of 2 **lemons**
8 cups **vegetable stock**
**sea salt** and **black pepper**

**To serve**
2 tablespoons chopped **parsley**
2 tablespoons **low-fat crème fraîche** or
    **plain yogurt** (optional)

Heat the olive oil in a large saucepan over medium heat, add the onions, and cook for 5 minutes, until softened. Add the ginger and garlic and cook for another 2 minutes.
......................................

Add the carrots, parsnips, and lemon zest and continue to cook for another 1–2 minutes. Pour in the stock and bring to a boil, then reduce the heat and simmer for about 20 minutes, until the carrots and parsnips are tender.
......................................

Put the soup in a blender or food processor, in batches if necessary, and blend until smooth. Return to the pan, stir in the lemon juice and season to taste. Heat through.
......................................

Serve the soup in warm bowls with a sprinkling of chopped parsley. Add a swirl of crème fraîche, if desired.
......................................

# BUTTERNUT SQUASH, ROSEMARY & LENTIL SOUP

Antioxidant-rich butternut squash is complemented by hormone-balancing lentils in this flavorsome soup.

**Preparation time:** 10 minutes
**Cooking time:** 1¼ hours
**Serves 4**
················

1 **butternut squash**, peeled, seeded, and diced
a few **rosemary sprigs**, plus extra to garnish
2 tablespoons **olive oil**
¾ cup **red lentils**, rinsed
1 **onion**, finely chopped
4 cups **vegetable stock**
**sea salt** and **black pepper**
**whole-wheat rolls**, to serve

Put the squash into a roasting pan with the rosemary, drizzle with the oil, and season to taste. Place in a preheated oven, at 400°F, for 45 minutes, until tender and golden.
··············································

Meanwhile, put the lentils into a saucepan and cover with water. Bring to a boil over high heat and cook rapidly for 10 minutes. Drain, then return the lentils to a clean saucepan with the onion and stock and simmer for 5 minutes. Season to taste.
··············································

Mash the butternut squash with a fork and add to the soup, discarding the rosemary. Simmer for 25 minutes or until the lentils are tender. Ladle the soup into warm bowls, garnish with rosemary sprigs, and serve with whole-wheat rolls.
··············································

# PEPPERED BEEF WITH SALAD GREENS

Beef is rich in iron to boost energy levels and fight fatigue, while mushrooms are rich in chromium to balance blood sugar.

**Preparation time:** 15 minutes
**Cooking time:** about 5 minutes
**Serves 4**

................

1 lb thick-cut **tenderloin steak**
3 teaspoons **mixed peppercorns**,
   coarsely crushed
1 cup **low-fat plain yogurt with live cultures**
1–1½ teaspoons **horseradish sauce**
1 **garlic clove**, crushed
5 cups **mixed salad greens**,
   including Romaine lettuce
1½ cups sliced **white button mushrooms**
1 **red onion**, thinly sliced
1 tablespoon **olive oil**
**sea salt** and **black pepper**

Trim the fat from the steak and rub the meat with the crushed peppercorns and some sea salt.

...............................

Mix the yogurt with the horseradish sauce and garlic and season to taste. Toss gently with the salad greens, mushrooms, and most of the red onion and divide among 4 serving plates.

.............................................................

Heat the oil in a skillet over high heat, add the steak, and cook for 2 minutes, until browned underneath. Turn over and cook for another 2 minutes for medium-rare steak, 3–4 minutes for medium, or 5 minutes for well done.

.............................................................

Slice the meat thinly and arrange the slices on top of the salads. Serve immediately, garnished with the remaining red onion.

.............................................................

# SUSHI RICE SALAD

This tasty salad is rich in nutrients that support weight loss, lift mood, and aid relaxation. Use seared tuna instead of raw salmon, if you prefer.

**Preparation time:** 20 minutes, plus cooling
**Cooking time:** 30 minutes
**Serves 4**

⅓ cup **rice wine vinegar**
2½ tablespoons **superfine** or
    **granulated sugar**
1 tablespoon finely chopped **Japanese
    pickled ginger**
½ teaspoons **wasabi paste**
½ **cucumber**
1⅓ cups **glutinous rice**
8 oz skinless, boneless **salmon**,
    cut into bite-size pieces
2 **avocados**, peeled, pitted, and cubed
8 **scallions**, finely sliced
¼ cup **toasted sesame seeds**

Put the vinegar and sugar into a small saucepan and heat gently, stirring, until the sugar has dissolved. Remove from the heat and add the pickled ginger and wasabi. Let cool.

Cut the cucumber in half lengthwise and scoop out the seeds with a teaspoon. Slice the flesh finely and add to the cooled vinegar.

Cook the rice according to package directions, then transfer to a bowl, strain the vinegar mixture over it, reserving the cucumber, stir, and let cool.

Transfer the cooled rice to a large salad bowl and toss gently with the reserved cucumber, salmon, avocado, and scallions. Sprinkle with toasted sesame seeds and serve immediately.

# LETTUCE WRAPPERS WITH CRAB

These delicious wrappers are low in saturated fat and calories, but they are guaranteed to lift the mood and assuage hunger.

**Preparation time:** 30 minutes
**Serves 4**
················

1 (1 lb) cooked **crab**
4 small **Romaine lettuce leaves**,
   hard stems removed

**Cucumber relish**
¼ **cucumber**, finely diced
3 **scallions**, thinly sliced
½ large **red chile**, seeded
   and finely chopped
2 tablespoons **cider vinegar**
1 teaspoon **light soy sauce**
1 teaspoon **superfine** or **granulated sugar**
4 teaspoons finely chopped fresh **cilantro**
   or **mint**
**sea salt** and **black pepper**

To make the relish, mix all the ingredients in a bowl and season to taste.
····················································

To prepare the crab, twist off the two large claws and the legs. Working on one leg or claw at a time, tap the shell with a rolling pin to break it, then use a small knife or skewer to remove all the white meat inside. Put into a bowl and set aside.
·············································································

Turn the crab body upside down on a board and press down hard on the undershell until it makes a cracking noise. Use your fingers to separate the top shell from the undershell. Scoop the brown meat from the top shell and put into the bowl with the leg and claw meat.
·········································································

Remove the pointed, spongy lungs from the top of the crab body, then pick all the white meat from the chambers, using a knife or rolling pin to break up the shell as necessary. Put the meat into the bowl and mix together the white and brown meats.
·················································································

When ready to serve, spoon the crab meat onto the lettuce leaves and top with the cucumber relish. Roll up and eat with the fingers.
·····················································

# SCALLOP, PARSNIP & CARROT SALAD

This creamy, high-fiber salad contains scallops to protect the heart, lower blood pressure, lift mood, and satisfy hunger.

**Preparation time:** 15 minutes
**Cooking time:** 25 minutes
**Serves 4**
...............

4 unpeeled **carrots**, quartered lengthwise
3 unpeeled **parsnips**, quartered lengthwise
2 tablespoons **olive oil**
1 tablespoon **cumin seeds**
12 large **scallops**
2 tablespoons **lemon juice**
**sea salt** and **black pepper**
chopped **parsley**, to garnish

**Dressing:**
⅓ cup **low-fat plain yogurt**
   **with live cultures**
2 tablespoons **lemon juice**
2 tablespoons **olive oil**
1 teaspoon **ground cumin**

Put the carrots and parsnips onto an aluminum foil-lined baking sheet, drizzle with half the oil, sprinkle with the cumin seed,s and season to taste. Place in a preheated oven, at 350°F, for 20–25 minutes, until tender.

......................................................

Meanwhile, make the dressing. Put all the ingredients into a small bowl, mix well, and season to taste.

......................................................

Trim the scallops to remove the tough muscle on the outside of the white fleshy part. Heat the remaining oil in a large skillet over high heat and cook the scallops for 2 minutes on each side until just cooked through. Drizzle with the lemon juice and transfer to a large bowl with any cooking juices.

......................................................

Add the carrots and parsnips to the bowl and toss together, then transfer to warm serving plates. Spoon the yogurt dressing over the top, garnish with parsley, and serve immediately.

......................................................

# GREEN BEAN & ASPARAGUS SALAD

This crunchy salad will help to banish belly fat, control high blood pressure, and boost the metabolism.

**Preparation time:** 10 minutes
**Cooking time:** 10 minutes
**Serves 4**

2 cups trimmed **green beans**
16 **asparagus spears**, trimmed
4 **eggs**
⅓ cup **olive oil**
1 tablespoon prepared **tapenade (black olive paste)**
1 tablespoon **balsamic vinegar**
3½ cups **arugula**
¾ cup pitted **black ripe olives**
3 oz **Parmesan cheese**, shaved
**sea salt** and **black pepper**

Cook the green beans in a steamer set over a saucepan of gently simmering water for 3 minutes. Add the asparagus and cook for another 5 minutes, until the vegetables are just tender.

Meanwhile, put the eggs in a small saucepan, cover with cold water, and bring quickly to a boil. Simmer for 2–3 minutes to soft boil, then drain, peel, and halve. Mix together the oil, tapenade, and vinegar in a small bowl and season to taste.

Divide the arugula leaves among 4 serving plates and top with the eggs. Arrange the beans and asparagus around the edge, then drizzle with the dressing. Sprinkle with the olives and Parmesan shavings and serve immediately.

# PUMPKIN, FETA & PINE NUT SALAD

Pumpkin is rich in fiber, antioxidants, and nutrients that help to regulate blood sugar, and feta is rich in calcium, which promotes relaxation.

**Preparation time:** 15 minutes
**Cooking time:** 25 minutes
**Serves 4**

4 cups peeled and seeded ¾ inch **pumpkin** or **butternut squash** cubes
1 tablespoon **olive oil**
2 **thyme sprigs**, coarsely chopped
1 (7 oz) package **mixed baby salad greens**
⅓ cup crumbled **feta cheese**
**sea salt** and **black pepper**

**Dressing**
1 teaspoon **Dijon mustard**
2 tablespoons **balsamic vinegar**
¼ cup **olive oil**

**To serve**
2 tablespoons **pine nuts**
2 tablespoons **pumpkin seeds**

Put the pumpkin into a roasting pan, drizzle with the oil, sprinkle with the thyme, and season to taste. Place in a preheated oven, at 375°F, for 25 minutes or until tender. Let cool slightly.

Meanwhile, whisk all the dressing ingredients together and season to taste. PUt the pine nuts and pumpkin seeds into a skillet over medium heat and dry-fry until lightly toasted.

Put the salad greens into a large bowl, add the cooked pumpkin, and sprinkle with the feta. Drizzle with the dressing and toss carefully to combine.

Divide the salad among 4 serving plates, sprinkle with the toasted pine nuts and pumpkin seeds, and serve immediately.

# RED PEPPER & FETA ROLLS WITH OLIVES

These tasty, Mediterranean rolls are chock-full of nutrients to support healthy weight loss and leave you looking and feeling great.

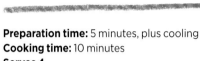

**Preparation time:** 5 minutes, plus cooling
**Cooking time:** 10 minutes
**Serves 4**
................

2 **red bell peppers**, cored, seeded
   and quartered lengthwise
⅔ cup crumbled **feta cheese**
16 **basil leaves**
16 pitted **black ripe olives**, halved
2 tablespoons **pine nuts**, toasted
1 tablespoon **prepared pesto**
1 tablespoon **prepared vinaigrette**

**To serve:**
3½ cups **arugula**
**whole-wheat crusty bread**
   (optional)

Arrange the red bell peppers, skin side up, on a baking sheet and place under a preheated hot broiler for 7–8 minutes, until the skins are blackened. Transfer the red peppers to a plastic bag, seal the top, and let cool for 20 minutes, then remove the skins.

................................

Lay the skinned red pepper quarters on a board and top with the feta, basil leaves, olives, and pine nuts. Carefully roll up the red peppers, secure with toothpicks, and divide among 4 serving plates.

................................................

Whisk the pesto with the vinaigrette and drizzle over the red pepper rolls. Serve with the arugula and whole-wheat crusty bread, if desired.

...................

# TUNA SKEWERS WITH COCONUT & MANGO SALAD

The fragrance and flavor of these zesty skewers alongside the fresh, antioxidant-rich salad are sublime.

**Preparation time:** 20 minutes, plus marinating
**Cooking time:** 5–10 minutes
**Serves 4**
................

1 inch piece of fresh **ginger root**, peeled and finely grated
4 **garlic cloves**, crushed
1 teaspoon **cayenne pepper**
1 teaspoon **ground coriander**
1 teaspoon **ground turmeric**
½ teaspoon **ground cinnamon**
finely grated zest of 1 **lime**
3 tablespoons **olive oil**
1¼ lb **tuna steaks**, cubed
**sea salt** and **black pepper**
chopped fresh **cilantro**, to serve

**Coconut & mango salad**
1½ cups **dried coconut flakes**
1 tablespoon **olive oil**
2 teaspoons **honey**
finely grated zest and juice of 1 **lime**
1 (7 oz) package **mixed salad greens**
2 ripe **mangoes**, peeled, pitted, and cubed
1 **avocado**, peeled, pitted, and cubed

Put 8 wooden skewers into a bowl of water and let soak. Meanwhile, put the ginger into a bowl with the garlic, cayenne pepper, ground coriander, turmeric, cinnamon, lime zest, oil, and ½ teaspoon of salt. Mix well, add the tuna, and toss to coat. Cover and marinate in the refrigerator for about an hour.

To make the salad, put the coconut flakes into a dry skillet over medium heat and toast for about 4 minutes, until just beginning to brown. Let cool.

To make the salad dressing, put the olive oil, honey, lime zest, and lime juice into a small bowl, season to taste, and mix well.

Thread the tuna onto the soaked skewers and place on an aluminum foil-lined baking sheet. Brush with the remaining marinade and place under a preheated hot broiler for 1–2 minutes on each side, until a little charred on the outside but still pink in the middle.

Put the salad greens into a large bowl and add the mango, coconut, and avocado. Drizzle with the dressing and toss well. Arrange the tuna skewers on serving plates, sprinkle with fresh cilantro, and serve with the salad.

# SMOKED HADDOCK WITH POACHED EGGS

Rich in protein to ease hunger and encourage healthy weight loss, this dish is quick to prepare and ideal for busy weeknights.

**Preparation time:** 10 minutes
**Cooking time:** about 20 minutes
**Serves 4**

1½ lb **new potatoes**
4 **scallions**, sliced
2 tablespoons **low-fat crème fraîche**
    or **plain yogurt**
½ bunch of **watercress**
4 (5 oz) **smoked haddock** or **other**
    **smoked fish fillets**
⅔ cup **skim milk**
1 **bay leaf**
4 **eggs**
**sea salt** and **black pepper**

Cook the potatoes in a saucepan of lightly salted boiling water for 12–15 minutes, until tender. Drain, lightly crush with a fork, then stir in the scallions, crème fraîche, and watercress and season to taste. Keep warm.

Meanwhile, put the fish and milk into a large skillet with the bay leaf. Bring to a boil over medium heat, then cover and simmer for 5–6 minutes until the fish is cooked through.

Bring a large saucepan of water to a gentle simmer. Carefully break 2 eggs into the water and cook for 3 minutes until the whites are just set. Remove with a slotted spoon and keep warm while cooking the remaining eggs.

Divide the potatoes among 4 serving plates and arrange the haddock on top. Top with the poached eggs and a sprinkling of black pepper and serve immediately.

# BAKED FISH WITH LEMON GRASS & GREEN PAPAYA SALAD

This Thai-inspired dish is low in calories and high in dieting power, with heart-supporting omega-3 oils.

**Preparation time:** 25 minutes
**Cooking time:** 20–25 minutes
**Serves 4**
................

4 (8 oz) whole **red snapper** or
    **mackerel**, gutted and scaled
4 **lemon grass stalks**,
    cut into 1 inch lengths
2 unpeeled **carrots**, cut into matchsticks
1½ tablespoons **light soy sauce**,
    plus extra to serve
2 tablespoons **lime juice**

**To serve**
small handful of chopped fresh **cilantro**
1 **red chile**, seeded and sliced
**lemon** wedges

**Green papaya salad**
2 **garlic cloves**, peeled
⅔ cup **roasted peanuts**
1 **green papaya**, peeled and finely shredded
1 cup **green beans** (1 inch pieces)
2 teaspoons **dried shrimp paste**
2 small fresh **Thai chiles**, finely chopped
2 tablespoons **honey**
1 tablespoon **Thai fish sauce**
finely grated zest and juice of 1 **lime**
8 **cherry tomatoes**

Put the fish into an ovenproof dish and use a sharp knife to score each side 3 or 4 times. Sprinkle with the lemon grass, carrots, soy sauce, and lime juice. Cover with aluminum foil and place in a preheated oven, at 350°F, for 20–25 minutes or until a the tip of a sharp knife can be inserted into the flesh without resistance.
.................................................

Meanwhile, make the salad with a large mortar and pestle. Put the garlic into the mortar and pound to break it up. Add the peanuts and pound coarsely. Add the papaya and pound softly, using a spoon to scrape down the sides, turning and mixing well.
.....................

Add the green beans and shrimp paste and keep pounding and turning to soften the beans. Add the chile, honey, fish sauce, lime juice, and lime zest and lightly pound together for another minute. Add the tomatoes and lightly pound for another minute. Taste and add more honey, fish sauce, lime juice, or chile, if needed; it should be a balance of sweet, sour, salty, and hot.
.................................................

Place the fish on warm serving plates and spoon the cooking juices over them. Sprinkle with chopped cilantro and sliced chile and serve with the green papaya salad, lemon wedges, and a small bowl of soy sauce.
.................................................

# CHICKEN BROCHETTES WITH CUCUMBER & KELP SALAD

A delicious combination of thyroid- and metabolism-boosting kelp with marinated, grilled chicken.

**Preparation time:** 20 minutes, plus soaking and marinating
**Cooking time:** 10 minutes
**Serves 4**

................

1 tablespoon **olive oil**, plus extra for brushing
finely grated zest and juice of 1 **lime**
2 teaspoons **dried oregano**
1 teaspoon **paprika**
4 boneless, skinless **chicken breasts**
**sea salt** and **black pepper**
**whole-wheat pita breads**, to serve

**Cucumber & kelp salad**
2 oz **dried kelp**, cut into strips
juice of 1 **lime**
1 large **cucumber**, thinly sliced
1 tablespoon **rice vinegar**
½ teaspoon **cider vinegar**
1 tablespoon **sesame oil**
2 teaspoons **coconut palm sugar** or **brown sugar**
2 tablespoons **toasted sesame seeds**
2 **scallions**, thinly sliced

At least 10 hours before you want to serve this dish, put the kelp into a large bowl with the lime juice and enough water to cover and set aside to soak. If the water has been fully absorbed after 3–4 hours, add more to cover again. The kelp will expand to about 5 times its original size.

................

Meanwhile, put the olive oil, lime zest, lime juice, oregano, and paprika into a bowl, season to taste, and stir well. Add the chicken and stir to coat, cover, and refrigerate for at least 2 hours, stirring again from time to time. Put 4 wooden skewers into a bowl of water and let soak.

................

Rinse and drain the kelp and put into a large bowl with the cucumber, vinegars, oil, and sugar, mix well, and set aside.

................

Cut the chicken into bite-size pieces and thread onto the skewers. Put the skewers onto an aluminum foil-lined baking sheet and brush with the remaining marinade. Place under a preheated hot broiler for about 5 minutes on each side, brushing with a little olive oil, if required, until browned and cooked through.

................

Stir the sesame seeds and onions into the salad and serve with the chicken brochettes and some whole-wheat pita breads.

................

# CHICKEN & BLUEBERRY PASTA SALAD

This filling salad will not only keep you going through the evening, but will encourage restful sleep as well.

**Preparation time:** 10 minutes
**Cooking time:** 20 minutes
**Serves 4**
...............

4 boneless, skinless **chicken breasts**
finely grated zest and juice of 2 **limes**
2 tablespoons chopped **thyme**
8 oz **whole-wheat** or **spelt penne**
3 tablespoons **olive oil**
3 **shallots**, peeled and diced
½ cup **chicken stock**
⅔ cup crumbled **feta cheese**
⅔ cup **blueberries**
2 **celery sticks**, finely chopped
3½ cups **arugula**
**sea salt** and **black pepper**

Place the chicken breasts in a large saucepan and cover with water. Add half the lime zest and half the thyme and bring to a boil over medium heat. Reduce the heat and simmer gently for about 10 minutes, or until just cooked through. Drain and let cool a little.

Meanwhile, cook the pasta in a saucepan of lightly salted boiling water according to package directions until tender but still with a little bite. Drain and put into a large bowl.

Heat the oil in a saucepan over medium heat, add the shallots, and cook for 2-3 minutes, or until softened. Stir in the stock, half the feta, and the lime juice, and cook until the feta melts into the stock.

Pour the sauce over the pasta in the bowl, then add the blueberries, celery, and the remaining lime zest and thyme. Season to taste, sprinkle with the remaining feta, and toss together to combine.

Arrange the arugula on a large plate and top with the pasta. Serve warm or cold.

# CHICKEN & APPLE STEW

This winning combination of nutty buckwheat, warming spices, and fresh apples balances blood sugar and encourages a good night's sleep.

**Preparation time:** 20 minutes
**Cooking time:** 50 minutes
**Serves 4**

⅔ cup **buckwheat**
2 tablespoons **olive oil**
¾ cup chopped **almonds**
1 teaspoon **cinnamon**
1 teaspoon **allspice**
1 teaspoon **ground cumin**
1 teaspoon **ground cardamom**
2 large **onions**, thinly sliced
4 large boneless, skinless **chicken thighs**
3 **Granny Smith** or **other cooking apples**, cored and cut into chunks
2 teaspoons chopped **thyme**
2 tablespoons **cider vinegar**
3 tablespoons **cider**
1¼ cups **chicken stock**
**sea salt** and **black pepper**
**green salad**, to serve

Cook the buckwheat in a saucepan of lightly salted boiling water according to package directions until tender. Drain and set aside.

Meanwhile, heat half the oil in a large skillet or wok over medium heat. Add the almonds and spices, season to taste, and cook until the almonds are well coated and beginning to caramelize. Transfer to a bowl and set aside.

Heat the remaining oil in the skillet over low heat and add the onions. Sauté for about 15 minutes, until soft and beginning to brown. Add the chicken and cook for 5 minutes, until lightly browned all over. Add the apples and cook for another 5 minutes, then stir in the thyme.

Add the cider vinegar, cider, and stock, increase the heat, and bring to a boil. Reduce the heat and simmer for about 20 minutes, until the chicken is cooked through and the apples are beginning to break up.

Stir in the buckwheat and almonds, season to taste, and warm through. Serve in warm bowls with a green salad.

# ROMAN CHICKEN WITH BELL PEPPERS

Bursting with Mediterranean flavors and packed with fiber and chromium, this tasty chicken dish will leave you feeling satisfied.

**Preparation time:** 15 minutes
**Cooking time:** 30 minutes
**Serves 4**

3 tablespoons **olive oil**
4 boneless, skinless **chicken breasts**
1 **red onion**, sliced
3 **garlic cloves**, finely chopped
2 **red bell peppers**, cored, seeded, and sliced
1 **yellow bell pepper**, cored, seeded, and sliced
1 **green bell pepper**, cored, seeded, and sliced
1½ cups sliced **white button mushrooms**
1 cup **pitted green olives**
1 (14½ oz) can **cherry tomatoes** or **diced tomatoes**
1¼ cups **chicken stock**
2 **oregano sprigs**
2 tablespoons chopped **parsley**
**sea salt** and **black pepper**
**brown rice**, to serve

Heat the oil in large, heavy saucepan over high heat, add the chicken, and brown all over. Remove from the pan and set aside.

Add the onion and garlic to the pan and cook for 1–2 minutes. Add the bell peppers and mushrooms and cook for another 2–3 minutes, then add the olives, cherry tomatoes, stock, and oregano.

Return the chicken to the pan, cover, and bring to a boil. Reduce the heat and simmer for about 20 minutes, until the chicken is cooked through. Stir in the parsley, season to taste, and serve with a little brown rice.

# LAMB & APRICOT STEW WITH PEARL BARLEY

Fragrant and tasty, this stew contains a host of nutrients to balance hormones, boost mood, and jump-start the metabolism.

**Preparation time:** 15 minutes
**Cooking time:** 1¼ hours
**Serves 4**

olive oil spray
1¼ lb lean diced **lamb**
1 **red onion**, chopped
1 unpeeled **carrot**, chopped
1 teaspoon **paprika**
1 teaspoon **ground coriander**
1 teaspoon **fennel seeds**
1¼ inch **cinnamon stick**
2 **garlic cloves**, crushed
2 **bay leaves**
3 tablespoons **lime juice**
3¼ cups **chicken stock**
⅔ cup **dried apricots**
1 (14½ oz) can **diced tomatoes**
⅓ cup **pearl barley**
⅓ cup chopped fresh **cilantro**,
    plus extra to garnish
1 cup **couscous**
**sea salt** and **black pepper**

Heat a large, heavy saucepan over high heat, spray lightly with oil, and cook the lamb briefly, in batches if necessary, until browned all over. Remove from the pan with a slotted spoon and set aside.

Add the onion and carrot to the pan and cook briefly until golden. Return the lamb to the pan, stir in the spices, garlic, bay leaves, two-thirds of the lime juice, the stock, apricots, tomatoes, and barley.

Season to taste, cover, and bring to a boil. Reduce the heat and simmer for 1 hour or until the lamb is tender. Stir in the cilantro and remaining lime juice.

Meanwhile, prepare the couscous according to package directions. Serve the hot stew with the couscous, garnished with fresh cilantro.

# CHEESY PORK WITH PARSNIP PUREE

Bound to satisfy even the heartiest appetite, these lean, cheesy pork cutlets are deliciously creamy.

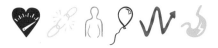

**Preparation time:** 15 minutes
**Cooking time:** 20 minutes
**Serves 4**
................

4 (4 oz) **lean pork loin cutlets**
1 teaspoon **olive oil**
⅓ cup crumbled **feta cheese**
   or ½ cup shredded **cheddar cheese**
½ tablespoon chopped **sage**
1½ cups fresh **whole-wheat bread crumbs**
1 **egg yolk**, beaten
5 unpeeled **parsnips**, chopped
2 **garlic cloves**, peeled
3 tablespoons **low-fat crème fraîche**
   or **plain yogurt**
**sea salt** and **black pepper**
steamed **green beans**, to serve

Season the pork cutlets with a little salt and plenty of black pepper. Heat the oil in a nonstick skillet over high heat, add the pork, and cook for 2 minutes on each side until browned, then transfer to an ovenproof dish.

.......................................

Put the cheese into a bowl with the sage, bread crumbs, and egg yolk. Mix well and divide the mixture into 4 portions. Use to top the pork cutlets, pressing down gently. Place in a preheated oven, at 400°F, for 12–15 minutes until the topping is golden and the pork is cooked through.

.......................................

Meanwhile, cook the parsnips and garlic in a saucepan of lightly salted boiling water for 10–12 minutes, until tender. Drain and mash with the crème fraîche and plenty of black pepper. Serve with the pork cutlets and some steamed green beans.

.......................................

# SLOW-COOKED SPICY BEEF

Meltingly tender beef with warming, digestion-boosting, fat-burning spices—this is a hearty meal in a bowl.

**Preparation time:** 20 minutes
**Cooking time:** 2¼ hours
**Serves 4-6**

....................

1 tablespoon **peanut oil**
1 large **onion**, chopped
1½ lb **boneless beef chuck**, cubed
2 tablespoons **tomato paste**
3 **tomatoes**, chopped
1 cup **water**
3 tablespoons **low-fat plain yogurt**
    **with live cultures**, plus extra to serve
1 teaspoon **nigella seeds**
**sea salt** and **black pepper**
**whole-wheat naan**, to serve

**Spice paste**
2 teaspoons **cumin seeds**
1 teaspoon **coriander seeds**
½ teaspoon **fennel seeds**
1 teaspoon **ground cinnamon**
2 **garlic cloves**, chopped
1 tablespoon grated **fresh ginger root**
1-2 small **green chiles**
1 teaspoon **paprika**
1 teaspoon **ground turmeric**
2 tablespoons **tomato paste**
2 tablespoons **peanut oil**
1 cup **cilantro** leaves,
    plus extra to garnish

To make the spice paste, dry-fry the cumin, coriander, and fennel seeds in a small skillet over medium heat for 2–3 minutes, until fragrant. Transfer the contents of the pan to a mini blender and blend to a fine powder. Add the remaining spice paste ingredients and blend until smooth.

.............................................

Heat the oil in a large saucepan over medium heat, add the onion, and sauté for 5–6 minutes or until beginning to brown, stirring occasionally. Add 3 tablespoons of the spice paste and stir-fry for 1–2 minutes.

.............................................................................

Stir in the meat and cook for 4–5 minutes or until the meat is browned and well coated. Stir in the tomato paste, tomatoes, measured water, and yogurt and bring to a boil. Reduce the heat, cover, and simmer for 2 hours or until tender, adding more liquid, if necessary.

.............................................

Season to taste and ladle into warm bowls. Sprinkle with the nigella seeds and garnish with cilantro leaves. Serve hot with naan and yogurt.

.............................................

# MOROCCAN CHICKPEAS WITH CARROTS & DATES

This meal is bursting with nutrients that support weight loss and, most importantly, it's delicious and satisfying.

**Preparation time:** 10 minutes
**Cooking time:** 30 minutes
**Serves 4**
...............

1 tablespoon **olive oil**
2 large **onions**, sliced
2 **garlic cloves**, sliced
2 large unpeeled **carrots**, sliced
1 large unpeeled **parsnip**, sliced
4 teaspoons **ground cumin**
2 teaspoons **ground turmeric**
1 teaspoon **ground cinnamon**, plus
    extra to serve
1 inch piece of fresh **ginger root**,
    peeled and finely grated
1 cup **vegetable stock**
1 (28 oz) cans **diced tomatoes**
2 (15 oz) cans **chickpeas**,
    rinsed and drained
⅔ cup pitted and coarsely
    chopped **dried dates**
1 tablespoon **honey**
finely grated zest and juice of ½ **lemon**
**sea salt** and **black pepper**

**To serve**
½ cup **slivered almonds**, lightly toasted
⅔ cup chopped fresh **cilantro**

Heat the oil in a large, heavy saucepan over medium heat and add the onions. Sauté for 5–10 minutes, until soft and starting to brown. Add the garlic and cook for another 1 minute, then stir in the carrots and parsnip.
...............

Add the cumin, turmeric, cinnamon, and ginger and mix well to coat the vegetables. Pour in the stock and tomatoes and bring to a boil.
...............

Add the chickpeas and dates, reduce the heat, and simmer, uncovered, for about 15 minutes, until the vegetables are tender.
...............

Add the honey, lemon zest, and lemon juice and season to taste. Serve in warm bowls, sprinkled with the almonds, fresh cilantro, and a little extra cinnamon.
...............

# VEGETABLE & TOFU STIR-FRY

The tofu in this quick-and-easy dinner is rich
in phytoestrogens to help balance hormones.

**Preparation time:** 15 minutes
**Cooking time:** 10 minutes
**Serves 4**
...............

3 tablespoons **sunflower oil**
10 oz **firm tofu**, cubed
1 **onion**, sliced
2 unpeeled **carrots**, sliced
2 cups small **broccoli** florets
1 **red bell pepper**, cored, seeded, and sliced
1 large **zucchini**, sliced
2 cups **sugar snap peas**
2 tablespoons **dark soy sauce**
2 tablespoons **sweet chili sauce**
½ cup **water**

**To garnish**
chopped **red chiles**
**Thai basil leaves**

Heat 1 tablespoon of the oil in a wok or
large skillet until starting to smoke, add
the tofu, and stir-fry over high heat for
2 minutes or until golden all over. Remove
with a slotted spoon and keep warm.
..............................................................

Heat the remaining oil in the pan, add
the onion and carrots, and stir-fry for
1½ minutes. Add the broccoli and red bell
pepper and stir-fry for 1 minute, then
add the zucchini and sugar snap peas
and stir-fry for 1 minute.
..............................................................

Mix together the soy sauce, chili sauce,
and measured water and add to the pan
with the tofu. Cook for another 1 minute.
Serve in warm bowls, garnished with
chopped red chiles and Thai basil leaves.
..............................................................

# PUMPKIN CURRY
# WITH PINK GRAPEFRUIT SALAD

This tasty curry is rich in antioxidants to support general health and helps combat the symptoms of stress, including low energy.

**Preparation time:** 20 minutes
**Cooking time:** 25 minutes
**Serves 4**

................

1 tablespoon **olive oil**
1 large **onion**, finely chopped
2 **garlic cloves**, finely chopped
1 teaspoon **ground coriander**
1 teaspoon **ground cumin**
2 teaspoons **ground turmeric**
1 teaspoon **curry powder**
½ inch piece of fresh **ginger root**, peeled and finely grated
1 teaspoon **black mustard seeds**
3¼ cups **vegetable stock**
1 cup **coconut milk**
6 cups peeled and seeded **pumpkin** or **butternut squash** chunks
**sea salt** and **black pepper**
⅔ cup chopped fresh **cilantro**, to serve

**Pink grapefruit salad**
4 **pink grapefruit**
1 tablespoon **olive oil**
2 **scallions**, finely chopped
1 tablespoon **honey**
finely grated zest and juice of ½ **lime**
1 cup fresh **mint** leaves
½ cup **almonds**, lightly toasted and chopped
1¼ cups chopped fresh **cilantro**

Heat the olive oil in a large saucepan over medium heat and add the onion. Sauté for about 5 minutes, until softened, then add the garlic and cook for another 2 minutes.

..................................................................

Add the ground coriander, cumin, turmeric, curry powder, ginger, and mustard seeds, stir well to combine, then pour in the stock and coconut milk. Bring to a boil and add the pumpkin. Reduce the heat and simmer, covered, for 10 minutes, until the pumpkin is tender.

..................................................

Meanwhile, prepare the salad by peeling the grapefruit with a sharp knife. Holding the grapefruit over a bowl to catch the juices, remove the segments by cutting between the membranes with the knife. Arrange the segments on a serving plate and set aside.

..................................................................

Put the oil, scallions, honey, lime zest, and lime juice into the bowl with the grapefruit juice, season to taste, and mix well. Drizzle the dressing over the grapefruit segments and sprinkle with the mint, almonds, and cilantro.

..................................................

Uncover the curry and cook for another 4–5 minutes to thicken the sauce. Sprinkle with the cilantro and serve with the pink grapefruit salad.

.......................

# THAI RED VEGETABLE CURRY

A spicy, creamy curry to lift mood, boost energy, balance blood sugar, aid digestion, and enhance the metabolism. For an extra boost, serve this curry with coconut rice.

**Preparation time:** 20 minutes, plus standing
**Cooking time:** 1 hour
**Serves 4**

1 tablespoon **peanut oil**, plus extra
    for greasing
1 large **onion**, chopped
1 small **sweet potato**, peeled and cubed
¼ **butternut squash**, peeled, seeded,
    and cut into cubes
1¾ cups **coconut milk**
1 cup **vegetable stock**
2 large **zucchini**, cut into chunks
1 cup trimmed **green beans**
1 (15 oz) can **chickpeas**
1 cup canned or cooked **green lentils**
handful of fresh **cilantro**, to serve
**plain** or **coconut rice**, to serve

**Curry paste**
2 teaspoons **cumin seeds**
2 teaspoons **coriander seeds**
1 teaspoon **ground turmeric**
3 **red chiles**, seeded
5 **scallions**, chopped
2 **garlic cloves**, chopped
1 inch piece of fresh **ginger root**,
    peeled and chopped
4 **lemon grass stalks**, outer leaves
    discarded, cores chopped
finely grated zest and juice of 1 **lime**
1 tablespoon **honey**

To make the spice paste, dry-fry the cumin and coriander seeds in a small skillet over medium heat for 2–3 minutes, until fragrant. Transfer the contents of the pan to a mini blender and blend to a fine powder. Add the remaining curry paste ingredients and blend until smooth, adding a little water if needed. Season with salt and black pepper.

Heat the peanut oil in a large saucepan over medium heat, add the onion, and cook for about 5 minutes, until just beginning to soften. Add 3–4 heaping tablespoons of the curry paste and cook for about another 5 minutes, until fragrant.

Add the sweet potato and squash and stir to coat, then pour in the coconut milk and stock. Bring to a boil, reduce the heat, and simmer for about 10 minutes until the vegetables are almost tender.

Add the zucchini, green beans, and the rinsed and drained chickpeas and lentils, and cook for another 10 minutes, until the zucchini are just cooked.

Sprinkle with chopped fresh cilantro and serve with rice. To make coconut rice, substitute a can of low-fat coconut milk for some of the cooking water.

# CHOCOLATE ESPRESSO DESSERTS

Dark chocolate boosts energy, balances mood, and reduces cravings. However, these desserts do contain saturated fat, so save them for a treat.

**Preparation time:** 5 minutes, plus chilling
**Cooking time:** 5 minutes
**Serves 4**
·················

4 oz **semisweet dark chocolate**,
   broken into small pieces
2 teaspoons **instant espresso powder**
⅔ cup **heavy cream**
¾ cup **low-fat Greek yogurt**
   **with live cultures**
4 **dark chocolate-coated coffee beans**,
   to decorate

Put 4 espresso cups or ramekins into the refrigerator to chill. Meanwhile, put the chocolate, espresso powder, and 3 tablespoons of the cream into a heatproof bowl set over a saucepan of gently simmering water, making sure the water does not touch the bottom of the bowl.
·················

Heat, stirring from time to time, until the chocolate has melted. Remove from the heat, stir in the remaining cream and half the yogurt, and pour into the chilled cups or ramekins.
·················

Spoon the remaining yogurt on top and decorate each portion with a coffee bean. Chill in the refrigerator for at least 10 minutes before serving.
·················

# CHOCOLATE-DIPPED CHERRIES

Cherries are wonderful for boosting metabolism and lifting mood; they are particularly delicious with dark chocolate.

**Preparation time:** 10 minutes, plus setting
**Cooking time:** 5 minutes
**Serves 4–6**

4 oz **bittersweet chocolate**, broken into small pieces
1½ cups unpitted **cherries** with stems, rinsed and dried

Put the chocolate into a heatproof bowl set over a saucepan of gently simmering water, making sure the water does not touch the bottom of the bowl. Heat, stirring from time to time, until the chocolate has melted. Remove the bowl from the heat and let cool slightly.

Hold the cherries by their stems, one by one, and dip into the chocolate, swirling them a little to get an even coverage. Transfer to a tray lined with parchment paper and let stand for 10–20 minutes to set.

# ALMOND & APPLE CAKE WITH VANILLA YOGURT

This cake is bursting with nutrients that encourage weight loss. A little goes a long way, so serve in small portions.

**Preparation time:** 20 minutes, plus cooling
**Cooking time:** about 1 hour
**Makes 16 slices**

1¾ sticks **butter**, softened,
    plus extra for greasing
4 **Granny Smith apples**, peeled,
    cored, and cut into chunks
1 cup **granulated sugar**
3 extra-large **eggs**, beaten
3–4 tablespoons **apple juice**
1¼ cups **whole-wheat flour**
¾ cup **ground almonds**
1¼ cups **baking powder**

**To serve**
2 cups **low-fat Greek yogurt**
    **with live cultures**
a few drops of **vanilla extract**

Grease an 8 inch round cake pan and line the bottom with parchment paper.

Melt 1 tablespoon of the butter in a large saucepan over medium heat and stir in the apples. Cook for about 5 minutes, until softened but still maintaining their shape. Remove from the heat and let cool.

Place the remaining butter and the sugar in a large bowl and beat until light and fluffy. Stir in the eggs, one at a time, beating constantly, then add the apple juice.

Sift the flour into the bowl, then add the bran out of the strainer with the ground almonds, baking powder, and half the apples. Fold the ingredients gently to combine.

Transfer the batter to the prepared cake pan, smooth, and top with the remaining apples, pushing them down into the batter so the tops are just showing.

Place in a preheated oven, at 350°F, for 55–60 minutes, until a toothpick inserted into the center of the cake comes out clean. Let cool in the pan.

Put the yogurt into a bowl and stir in the vanilla. Serve with the cake.

# BLUEBERRY CHEESECAKE DESSERTS

Filled with dairy produce and fat-busting blueberries, these creamy little deconstructed cheesecakes are quick and simple to make.

**Preparation time:** 20 minutes, plus cooling and chilling
**Cooking time:** 5 minutes
**Serves 4**

1⅓ cups **blueberries**
1 teaspoon **honey**
8 **amaretti cookies**
2 tablespoons **unsalted butter**, melted
⅔ cup **reduced-fat cream cheese**
⅔ cup **low-fat Greek yogurt with live cultures**
¼ cup **confectioners' sugar**
finely grated zest and juice of 1 **lemon**

Put the blueberries into a small saucepan over low heat and stir in the honey. Bring to a gentle simmer and cook for about 5 minutes, until the blueberries are bursting and their juices running. Remove from the heat and let cool.

Put the amaretti cookies into a food processor and blend to a fine crumb. Add the melted butter and pulse until moist and well combined. Press the mixture into the bottoms of 4 individual serving glasses.

Put the cream cheese, yogurt, sugar, lemon zest, and lemon juice into a bowl and beat until fluffy and well combined.

Divide the mixture among the 4 glasses, then top with the blueberry mixture. Chill in the refrigerator for 20–30 minutes before serving.

# COCONUT MANGO PUDDING

With a host of healthy nutrients, this mango pudding
is utterly delicious, easy to make, and surprisingly light.

**Preparation time:** 15 minutes, plus chilling
**Cooking time:** 2 minutes
**Serves 4**
................

2 large ripe **mangoes**, peeled,
  pitted, and cut into chunks
4 **sheets of gelatin**
½ cup hot **water**
⅓ cup **honey**
1¾ cups **coconut milk**
**mint sprigs**, to decorate

Put the mango chunks into a blender
or food processor and blend until
smooth. Put the gelatin sheets into
a small bowl, cover with cold water,
and let soak for a few minutes.
..........................................................

Put the measured hot water and honey
into a small saucepan over medium heat
until boiling, then remove from the heat.
Squeeze any excess water from the
gelatin sheets and drop them into
the saucepan, one at a time, stirring
well after each addition to dissolve.
..........................................................

Pour the mixture into the blender
or food processor with the mango,
add the coconut milk, and blend until
smooth and well combined. Pour into
individual serving glasses and chill in
the refrigerator for about 2 hours, until
set. Serve decorated with mint sprigs.
..........................................................

# BAKED APPLES

Rich in fiber and packed with crunchy, filling oats and walnuts, this dessert is satisfying and easy to make.

**Preparation time:** 10 minutes
**Cooking time:** 25 minutes
**Serves 4**
................

4 **sweet crisp apples**
⅓ cup **maple syrup**, plus extra for drizzling
¾ cup **steel-cut oats**
½ cup chopped **walnuts**
1 tablespoon **ground cinnamon**
**low-fat Greek yogurt with
  live cultures**, to serve

Cut the apples in half lengthwise and use a small knife to cut out the cores to leave a cavity in the center of each apple half. Place the halves, cut side up, on a baking sheet lined with parchment paper.

Put the maple syrup, oats, and walnuts into a bowl and stir until well combined. Press the mixture into the cavities in the apples, then sprinkle generously with cinnamon.

Drizzle with a little more maple syrup and place in a preheated oven, at 350°F, for 25 minutes, or until the apples are soft but still holding their shape. Serve warm with Greek yogurt.

# GREEN TEA & GINGER GRANITA

This is a light and refreshing way to end a hearty meal,
with warming ginger and antioxidant-rich green tea.

**Preparation time:** 15 minutes,
   plus cooling and freezing
**Cooking time:** 5 minutes
**Serves 4**
················

3 cups **water**
2 tablespoons **granulated sugar**
2 tablespoons **honey**
1 inch piece of **fresh ginger root**,
   peeled and finely chopped
5 **green tea bags**
finely grated zest and juice of ½ **orange**

Put the measured water into a large
saucepan over medium heat, add the sugar,
honey, ginger, tea bags, and orange zest,
and stir until the sugar has dissolved.
Remove from the heat and let cool.
·············································

Stir in the orange juice, then strain into
a shallow freezer-proof container. Put
into the freezer for 30 minutes, then break
up the ice crystals with a fork.
·········································

Freeze for another 45 minutes and
repeat. The granita is ready to serve
when it is completely frozen and
broken into shards of ice.
·······································

# SLICED ORANGES WITH ALMONDS

This delicious orange salad is high in fiber to balance blood sugar and encourage healthy digestion. Perfect for dessert or breakfast.

**Preparation time:** 10 minutes
**Serves 4**
················

8 **oranges**
1 tablespoon **confectioners' sugar**
1 teaspoon **ground cinnamon**
¾ cup chopped **almonds**

Peel 7 of the oranges with a sharp knife, removing most of the white pith with the peel. Slice the oranges into ½ inch thick circles and arrange on a serving plate.
··················································································

Sprinkle with the confectioners' sugar and drizzle with the zest and juice of the remaining orange. Sprinkle with the cinnamon and almonds and serve immediately.
··································································

# GRILLED PEACHES & APRICOTS WITH HONEY YOGURT

Rich in antioxidants and fiber, these fragrant fruits are softened and lightly caramelized on a grill pan for an unctuous dessert.

**Preparation time:** 10 minutes
**Cooking time:** about 5 minutes
**Serves 4**

2 tablespoons **vanilla sugar**
3 **peaches**, quartered and pitted
4 **apricots**, halved and pitted
1 cup **low-fat Greek yogurt
   with live cultures**
2 tablespoons **honey**

Put the sugar into a large bowl, add the fruit, and toss gently to coat.

Preheat a ridged grill pan until hot, then add the peaches, cut side down. Cook over medium heat for 2–3 minutes, until caramelized, then add the apricots. Turn over the peaches and cook for another 2–3 minutes, until all the fruit is soft.

Meanwhile, put the yogurt into a bowl and pour the honey over it. Stir briefly to create a rippled effect. Serve the warm, grilled fruit with the honey yogurt.

# CINNAMON BRIOCHE WITH MIXED BERRIES

These slices of French toast-style brioche are a little sinful, but happily balanced by antioxidant- and fiber-rich berries.

**Preparation time:** 10 minutes
**Cooking time:** 10 minutes
**Serves 4**

1 extra-large **egg**
2 teaspoons **ground cinnamon**
2 tablespoons **granulated sugar**
½ cup **skim milk**
1 tablespoon **olive oil**
4 slices of **brioche bread**
3 cups **mixed berries**, such as strawberries, raspberries, blueberries, and blackberries
**low-fat frozen yogurt**, to serve

Put the egg, cinnamon, and sugar into a shallow dish, whisk to combine, then whisk in the milk.

Heat a large skillet over medium heat and add half the olive oil. Dip 2 slices of brioche into the egg mixture, turning to coat evenly, then place in the hot skillet. Cook for 2–3 minutes on each side, until golden.

Remove the cooked brioche from the pan and keep warm. Repeat with the remaining slices, adding a little more oil if necessary.

Top the brioche with the mixed berries and serve with scoops of frozen yogurt.

# RESOURCES

**American Chronic Pain Association**
Tel: (800) 533-3231 (toll-free)
E-mail: ACPA@theacpa.org
Web site: www.theacpa.org

**American Diabetes Association**
Tel: (800) 342-2383 (toll-free)
E-mail: AskADA@diabetes.org
Web site: www.diabetes.org

**American Society for Nutrition**
Tel: (301) 634-7050
Web site: www.nutrition.org

**Anxiety and Depression Association of America**
Tel: (240) 485-1001
Web site: www.adaa.org

**The Better Sleep Council**
Tel: (703) 683-8371
Web site: www.bettersleep.org

**Black Women's Health Imperative**
Tel: (202) 548-4000
E-mail: info@BlackWomensHealth.org
Web site: www.blackwomenshealth.org

**Food and Nutrition Information Center**
Tel: (301) 504-5414
E-mail: FNIC@ars.usda.gov
Web site: fnic.nal.usda.gov

**Hepatitis Foundation International**
Tel: (800) 891-0707 (toll-free)
E-mail: info@hepatitisfoundation.org
Web site: www.hepatitisfoundation.org

**International Foundation for Functional Gastrointestinal Disorders**
Tel: (888) 964-2001 (toll-free)
Tel: (414) 964-1799 (local)
E-mail: iffgd@iffgd.org
Web site: www.iffgd.org

**Mental Health America**
Tel: (800) 969-6642 (toll-free)
Tel: (703) 684-7722 (local)
Web site: www.mentalhealthamerica.net

**National Alliance for Hispanic Health**
Tel: (202) 387-5000
E-mail: alliance@hispanichealth.org
Web site: www.hispanichealth.org

**National Alliance on Mental Illness**
Tel: (800) 950-6264 (toll-free)
Tel: (703) 524-7600 (local)
Web site: www.nami.org

**National Eating Disorders Association**
Tel: (800) 931-2237 (toll-free)
Tel: (206) 382-3587 (local)
E-mail: info@NationalEatingDisorders.org
Web site: www.nationaleatingdisorders.org

**National Institute of Mental Health**
Tel: (866) 615-6464 (toll-free)
Tel: (301) 443-4513 (local)
E-mail: nimhinfo@nih.gov
Web site: www.nimh.nih.gov/index.shtml

**National Sleep Foundation**
Tel: (703) 243-1697
E-mail: nsf@sleepfoundation.org
Web site: www.sleepfoundation.org

**National Women's Health Network**
Tel: (202) 682-2640
E-mail: healthquestion@nwhn.org
Web site: nwhn.org

**North American Menopause Society**
Tel: (800) 774-5342 (toll-free)
Tel: (440) 442-7550 (local)
E-mail: info@menopause.org
Web site: www.menopause.org

**North American Vegetarian Society**
Tel: (518) 568-7970
Web site: www.navs-online.org

**Society for Nutrition Education and Behavior**
Tel: (800) 235-6690 (toll-free)
Tel: (317) 328-4627 (local
E-mail: info@sne.org
Web site: www.sne.org

# INDEX

## Acknowledgments

Gill Paul would like to
thank the talented team
at Octopus: Denise
Bates, who came up
with the idea for the
series; Katy Denny, Alex
Stetter, and Jo Wilson,
who edited the books so
efficiently and made it
all work; and to the
design team of Jonathan
Christie and Isabel de
Cordova for making it all
look so gorgeous. Thank
you also to Karel Bata
for all the support and
for eating my cooking.

Karen Sullivan would
like to thank Cole, Luke,
and Marcus.

## Picture credits